A-Z NORTHAM[PTON] & WELLINGBO[ROUGH]

Key to Maps

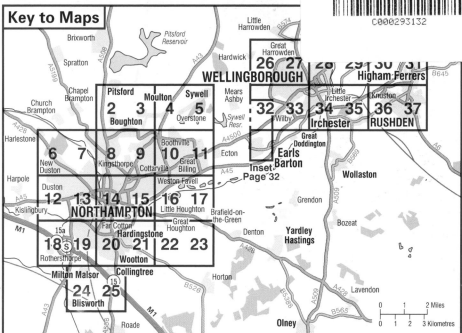

Reference

Motorway	**M1**
A Road	A428
Proposed	
B Road	B526
Dual Carriageway	
One Way Street — Traffic flow on A roads is indicated by a heavy line on the driver's left.	
Restricted Access	
Pedestrianized Road	
Track & Footpath	
Residential Walkway	

Railway — Level Crossing — Station	
Built Up Area	
Local Authority Boundary	
Postcode Boundary	
Map Continuation	8
Car Park Selected	P
Church or Chapel	†
Fire Station	■
Hospital	H
Information Centre	🄸
National Grid Reference	475

Police Station	▲
Post Office	★
Toilet	▽
with facilities for the Disabled	♿
Educational Establishment	
Hospital or Hospice	
Industrial Building	
Leisure or Recreational Facility	
Place of Interest	
Public Building	
Shopping Centre or Market	
Other Selected Buildings	

Scale 1:15,840

0 — ¼ — ½ Mile
0 — 250 — 500 — 750 Metres — 1 Kilometre

4 inches (10.16 cm) to 1 mile
6.31cm to 1kilometre

Geographers' A-Z Map Company Limited

Head Office :
Fairfield Road, Borough Green, Sevenoaks, Kent TN15 8PP
Telephone 01732 781000 (General Enquiries & Trade Sales)

Showrooms :
44 Gray's Inn Road, London WC1X 8HX
Telephone 020 7440 9500 (Retail Sales)
www.a-zmaps.co.uk

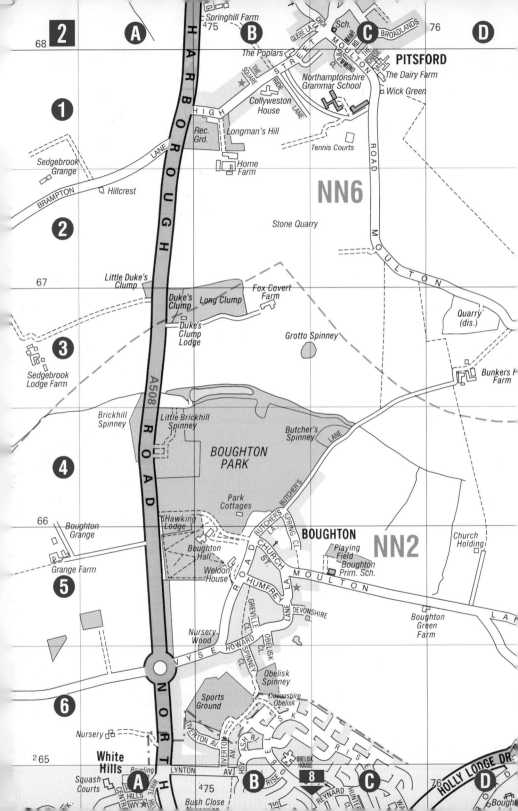

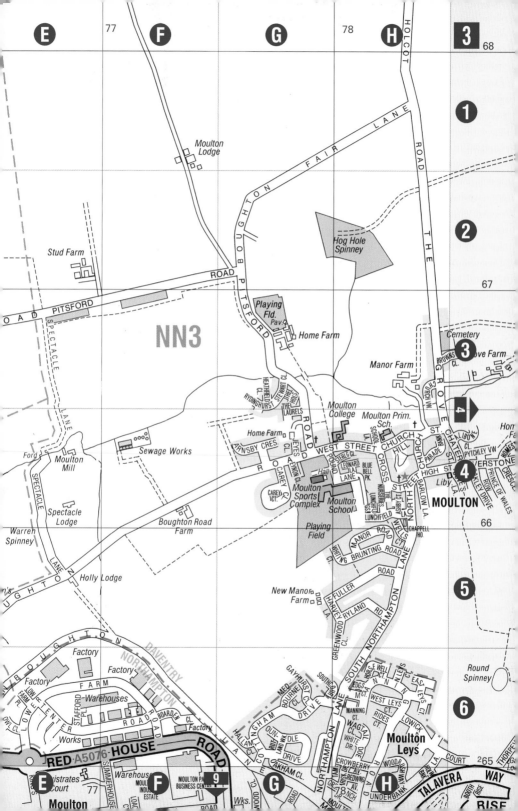

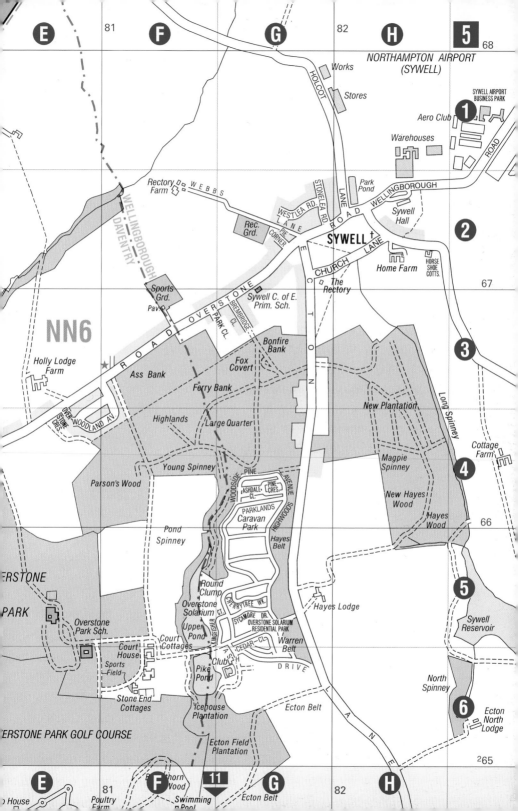

NORTHAMPTON AIRPORT
(SYWELL)

Works

Stores

SYWELL AIRPORT
BUSINESS PARK

Aero Club **1**

Warehouses

HOLCOT

STONELEA RD.

LANE

ROAD

WELLINGBOROUGH

Rectory
Farm

WEBBS

WESTLEA RD.

PIE

LANE

CORNER

Park
Pond

Rec.
Grd.

Sywell
Hall **2**

SYWELL

CHURCH LANE

Home Farm

HORSE
SHOE
COTTS.

67

Sports
Grd.
Pav.

OVERSTONE

PARK CL.

BREHMBRIDGE CL.

Sywell C. of E.
Prim. Sch.

The
Rectory

NN6

ROAD

Holly Lodge
Farm

Ass Bank

Fox
Covert

Bonfire
Bank

3

OVERSTONE CRES.

WOODLAND AV.

Ferry Bank

Highlands

Large Quarter

New Plantation

Long Spinney

Cottage
Farm

ERSTONE

PARK

Parson's Wood

Young Spinney

WOODSIDE

PINE

AVENUE

ASHDALE CL.

PINE CRES.

HIGHWOODS

SCHOOL

Magpie
Spinney

New Hayes
Wood

4

Hayes
Wood

66

Pond
Spinney

PARKLANDS
Caravan
Park

Hayes
Belt

Overstone
Park Sch.

Round
Clump

Overstone
Solarium

Upper
Pond

Court
Cottages

Court
House

Sports
Field

Stone End
Cottages

KINGFISHER CL.

CHERRYTREE WK.

SYCAMORE DR.

ASH CL.

CEDAR CL.

Club H.

Pike
Pond

DRIVE

Overstone Solarium
RESIDENTIAL PARK

Warren
Belt

Hayes Lodge

5

Sywell
Reservoir

North
Spinney

6

Ecton
North
Lodge

Icehouse
Plantation

Ecton Belt

ERSTONE PARK GOLF COURSE

Ecton Field
Plantation

Blackthorn Wood

11

Swimming Pool

Ecton Belt

265

House

Poultry
Farm

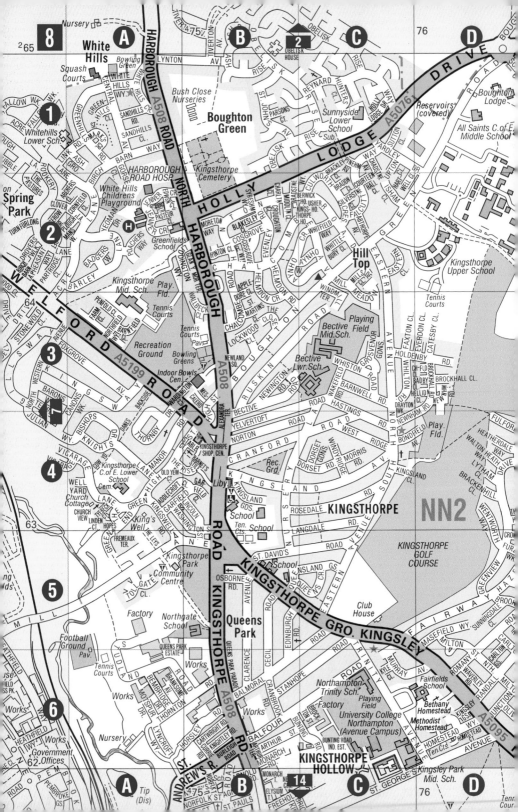

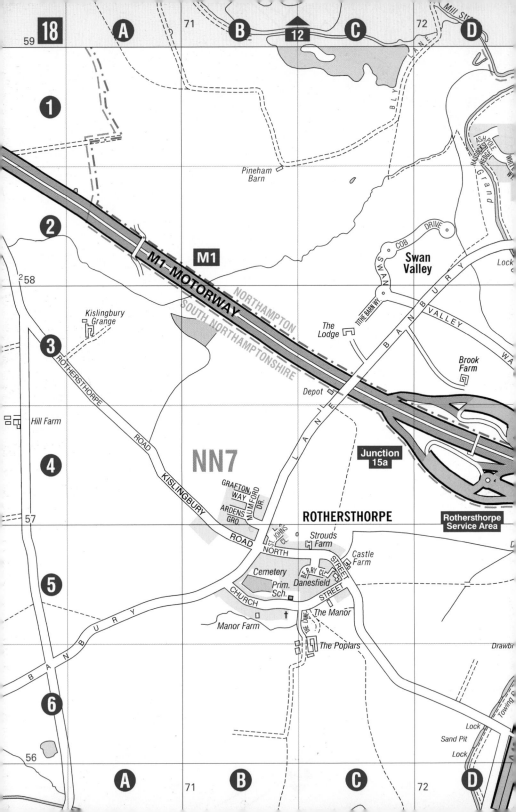

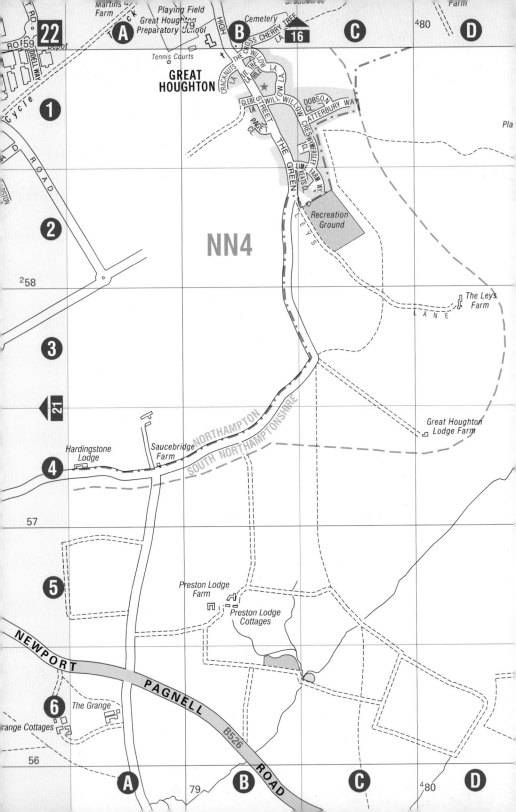

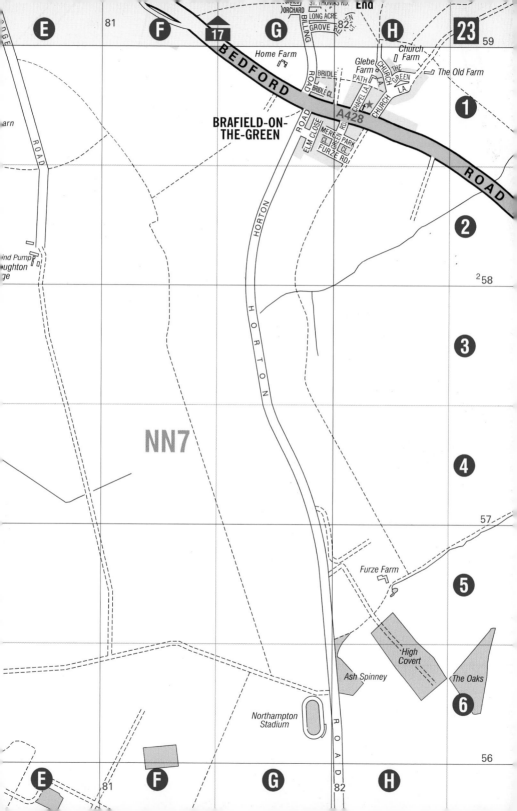

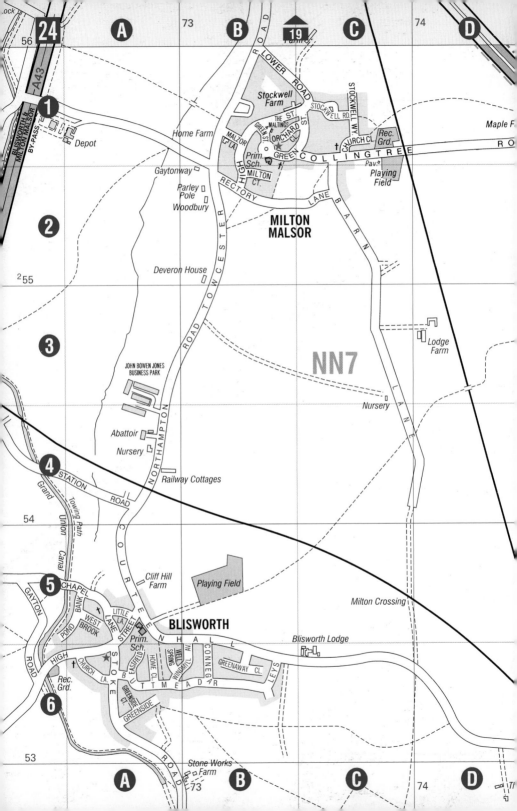

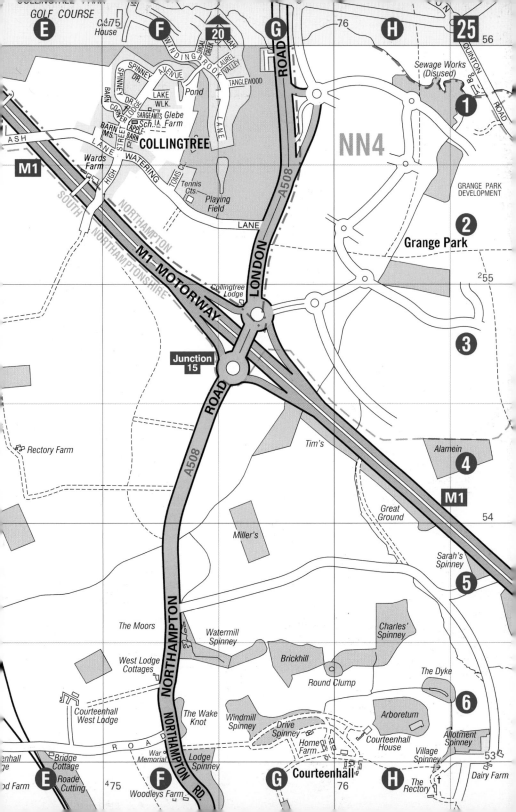

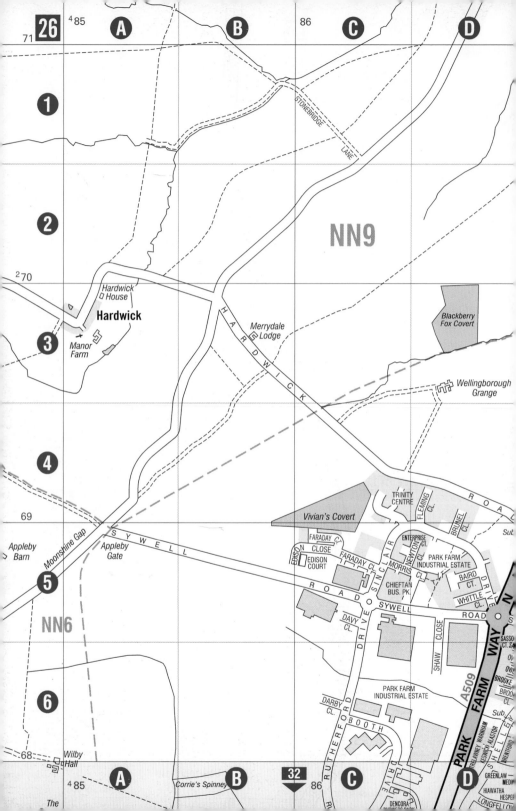

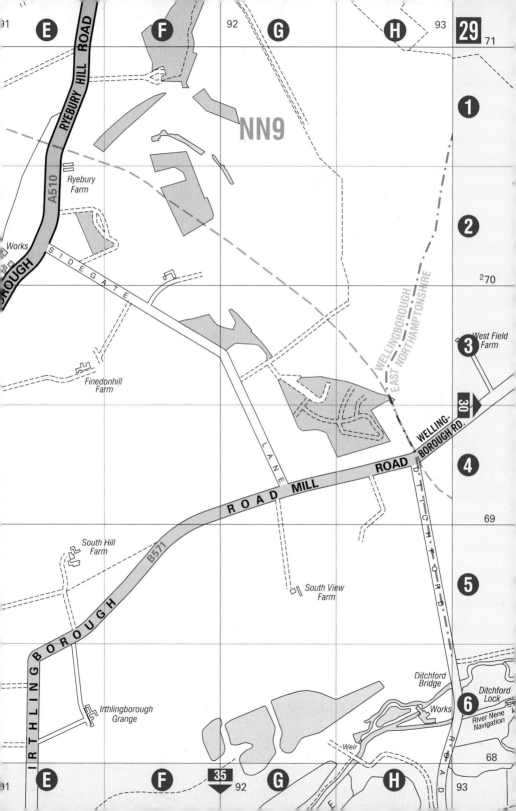

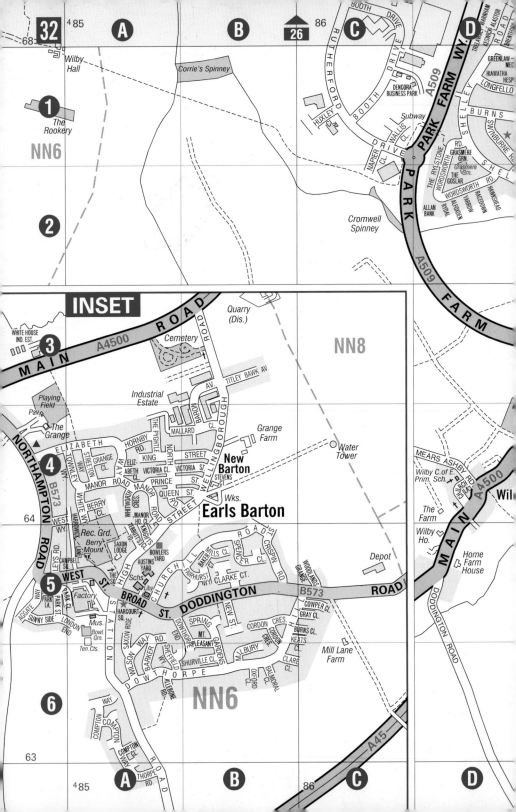

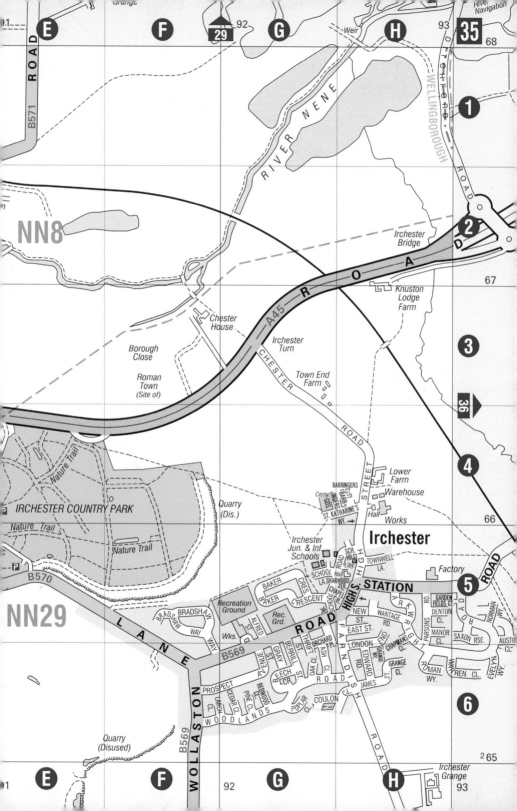

INDEX TO STREETS

Including Industrial Estates and a selection of Subsidiary Addresses.

HOW TO USE THIS INDEX

1. Each street name is followed by its Posttown or Postal Locality and then by its map reference; e.g. Abbey Rd. *Well* —2H **33** is in the Wellingborough Posttown and is to be found in square 2H on page **33**. The page number being shown in bold type.
   A strict alphabetical order is followed in which Av., Rd., St., etc. (though abbreviated) are read in full and as part of the street name; e.g. Ash Clo. appears after Ashby Gdns. but before Ashcroft Clo.

2. Streets and a selection of Subsidiary names not shown on the Maps, appear in the index in *Italics* with the thoroughfare to which it is connected shown in brackets; e.g. *Adelaide Ter. North* —1B **14** (off Barrack Rd.)

GENERAL ABBREVIATIONS

All : Alley	Cotts : Cottages	La : Lane	Ri : Rise
App : Approach	Ct : Court	Lit : Little	Rd : Road
Arc : Arcade	Cres : Crescent	Lwr : Lower	Shop : Shopping
Av : Avenue	Cft : Croft	Mc : Mac	S : South
Bk : Back	Dri : Drive	Mnr : Manor	Sq : Square
Boulevd : Boulevard	E : East	Mans : Mansions	Sta : Station
Bri : Bridge	Embkmt : Embankment	Mkt : Market	St : Street
B'way : Broadway	Est : Estate	Mdw : Meadow	Ter : Terrace
Bldgs : Buildings	Fld : Field	M : Mews	Trad : Trading
Bus : Business	Gdns : Gardens	Mt : Mount	Up : Upper
Cvn : Caravan	Gth : Garth	N : North	Va : Vale
Cen : Centre	Ga : Gate	Pal : Palace	Vw : View
Chu : Church	Gt : Great	Pde : Parade	Vs : Villas
Chyd : Churchyard	Grn : Green	Pk : Park	Wlk : Walk
Circ : Circle	Gro : Grove	Pas : Passage	W : West
Cir : Circus	Ho : House	Pl : Place	Yd : Yard
Clo : Close	Ind : Industrial	Quad : Quadrant	
Comn : Common	Junct : Junction	Res : Residential	

POSTTOWN AND POSTAL LOCALITY ABBREVIATIONS

Abing : Abington	*Far C* : Far Cotton	*K'thpe* : Kingsthorpe	*Roth* : Rothersthorpe
Blis : Blisworth	*Fin* : Finedon	*Kis* : Kislingbury	*Roth A* : Rothersthorpe Avenue Ind. Est.
Bou : Boughton	*Fin R* : Finedon Road Ind. Est.	*Knu* : Knuston	*Rou S* : Round Spinney Ind. Est.
Brac I : Brackmills Ind. Est.	*Graf S* : Grafton Street Ind. Est.	*L Bil* : Little Billing	*Rush* : Rushden
Braf G : Brafield on the Green	*Gt Bil* : Great Billing	*L Hou* : Little Houghton	*St James* : St James Bus. Pk.
Chap B : Chapel Brampton	*Gt Dod* : Great Doddington	*L Irch* : Little Irchester	*Sem* : Semilong
Clif : Cliftonville	*Gt Har* : Great Harrowden	*Lodge F* : Lodge Farm Ind. Est.	*Spin H* : Spinney Hill
Cog : Cogenhoe	*Gt Hou* : Great Houghton	*Mil M* : Milton Malsor	*Swan V* : Swan Valley
Col : Collingtree	*Hard* : Hardingstone	*Moul* : Moulton	*Syw* : Sywell
Cour : Courteenhall	*H'wck* : Hardwick	*Moul P* : Moulton Park	*Upton* : Upton
Crow L : Crow Lane Ind. Est.	*Harl* : Harlestone	*Moul I* : Moulton Park Ind. Est.	*Wee R* : Weedon Road Ind. Est.
Dal : Dallington	*Harp* : Harpole	*New D* : New Duston	*Well* : Wellingborough
Del : Delapre	*High F* : Higham Ferrers	*North* : Northampton	*West I* : Westgate Ind. Est.
Den I : Denington Ind. Est.	*Hort* : Horton	*Over* : Overstone	*W Fav* : Weston Favell
Dus : Duston	*Irch* : Irchester	*Park F* : Park Farm Ind. Est.	*Wilby* : Wilby
Earls B : Earls Barton	*Irth* : Irthlingborough	*Pit* : Pitsford	*Woot* : Wootton
Ecton : Ecton	*K Hth* : Kings Heath Ind. Est.	*Riv B* : Riverside Bus. Pk.	*Wym* : Wymington

INDEX TO STREETS

Abbey Lodge. *North* —2H **15**
Abbey Rd. *North* —6A **14**
Abbey Rd. *Well* —2H **33**
Abbey St. *North* —3H **13**
Abbey Way. *Rush* —5E **37**
Abbots Way. *North* —3G **13**
Abbots Way. *Well* —1H **33**
Abbotts Way. *Rush* —4D **36**
Aberdare Rd. *North* —1H **13**
Abington Av. *North* —1E **15**
Abington Cotts. *North* —1F **15**
Abington Ct. *North* —6G **9**
Abington Gro. *North* —1E **15**
Abington Pk. Cres. *North*
   —2G **15**
Abington Pl. *North* —3D **14**
Abington Sq. *North* —3C **14**
Abington St. *North* —3C **14**
Abthorpe Av. *North* —2C **8**
Acre La. *North* —2G **7**
Adams Av. *North* —2E **15**
Adams Clo. *Well* —6B **28**
Addington Rd. *Irth* —1D **30**
Addison Rd. *North* —5G **9**
Addlecroft Clo. *North* —4A **8**
Adelaide Pl. *North* —4B **14**
Adelaide St. *North* —2B **14**
Adelaide Ter. North —1B **14**
   (off Barrack Rd.)
Adit Vw. *Irth* —3C **30**
Adnitt Rd. *North* —2E **15**
Adnitt Rd. *Rush* —3E **37**
Agnes La. *North* —1B **14**
Ainsdale Clo. *North* —4E **9**
Aintree Rd. *North* —3E **9**
Alastor. *Well* —6D **26**
Albany Rd. *North* —2F **15**
Albert Pl. *North* —3C **14**
Albert Rd. *Rush* —3F **37**
Albert Rd. *Well* —5B **28**
Albion Ct. *North* —4C **14**

Albion Pl. *North* —4C **14**
Albion Pl. *Rush* —4F **37**
Alcombe Rd. *North* —2C **14**
Alcombe Ter. *North* —2D **14**
Alder Ct. *North* —2C **10**
Alderley Clo. *North* —1C **12**
Aldwell Clo. *Woot* —4E **21**
Alexander Ct. *North* —4B **10**
Alexandra Rd. *North* —3D **14**
Alexandra Rd. *Well* —5B **28**
Alexandra Ter. *North* —4B **8**
Alfoxden. *Well* —2D **32**
Alfred St. *Irch* —5G **35**
Alfred St. *North* —3E **15**
Alfred St. *Rush* —3F **37**
Alibone Clo. *Moul* —4A **4**
Allan Bank. *Well* —2D **32**
Allard Clo. *North* —2G **11**
Allebone Rd. *Earls B* —6A **32**
Allen Rd. *Irth* —2C **30**
Allen Rd. *North* —2E **15**
Allen Rd. *Rush* —2G **37**
Alley Yd. *North* —3B **14**
Alliance Ter. *Well* —6A **28**
Alliston Gdns. *North* —2B **14**
Alma St. *North* —3H **13**
Alma St. *Well* —6A **28**
Alpine Clo. *Rush* —3D **36**
Alpine Way. *North* —4B **6**
Alsace Clo. *North* —6A **6**
Althorp Clo. *Well* —4E **27**
Althorp Rd. *North* —3H **13**
Althorp St. *North* —3B **14**
Alton St. *North* —6A **14**
Alvis Ct. *North* —3F **11**
Ambleside Clo. *North* —3H **9**
Ambleside Clo. *Well* —6E **27**
Ambridge Clo. *Moul* —3G **19**
Ambush St. *North* —3A **14**
Anderson Grn. *North* —1E **33**
Andrew Clo. *High F* —4G **31**

Angel La. Well —1A **34**
   (off Silver St.)
Angel St. *North* —4B **14**
Anglia Way. *Moul I* —2E **9**
Anjou Ct. *New D* —5A **6**
Anne Clo. *High F* —4G **31**
Anne Rd. *Well* —3G **33**
Annesley Clo. *North* —3A **16**
Ansell Way. *Hard* —3D **20**
Applebarn Clo. *Col* —1F **25**
Appleby Clo. *North* —2H **27**
Appleby Wlk. *North* —3H **9**
Appledore Clo. *North* —3B **8**
Aquitaine Clo. *North* —6A **6**
Arbour Ct. *North* —3B **10**
Arbour Vw. Ct. *North* —2B **10**
Arbour Wlk. *North* —2B **10**
Archangel Rd. *North* —1F **19**
Archangel Sq. *North* —1G **19**
Archers Clo. *North* —2A **8**
Archfield. *Well* —1H **33**
Archfield Ter. Irth —1D **30**
   (off Lilley Ter.)
Archway Cotts. *North* —1F **15**
Ardens Gro. *Roth* —4B **18**
Ardington Rd. *North* —2F **15**
Argyle St. *North* —3H **13**
Ariel Clo. *North* —6B **6**
Arkwright Rd. *Irch* —5H **35**
Arlbury Rd. *North* —3D **10**
Arndale. *North* —2G **7**
Arnold Rd. *North* —1B **14**
Arrow Head Rd. *North* —6G **13**
Arthur St. *North* —6B **8**
Arthur St. *Well* —1G **33**
Arthur Ter. *North* —6B **8**
Artizan Rd. *North* —2E **15**
Arundel Ct. *Rush* —5E **37**
Arundel St. *North* —2B **14**
Ashbrow Rd. *North* —6G **13**

Ashburnham Rd. *North* —1E **15**
Ashby Clo. *Well* —4F **27**
Ashby Ct. *Moul* —4H **3**
Ashby Dri. *Rush* —5E **37**
Ashby Gdns. Moul —4H **3**
   (off Ashby Ct.)
Ash Clo. *Irch* —6G **35**
Ashcroft Clo. *North* —6C **6**
Ashcroft Gdns. *North* —5F **9**
Ashdale Clo. *Syw* —4G **5**
Ash Dri. *Syw* —6G **5**
Ashes, The. *Woot* —5G **21**
Ashfield Rd. *Well* —1G **33**
Ashford Clo. *North* —3H **15**
Ash Gro. *North* —1A **8**
Ash La. *Col* —1E **25**
Ashley La. *Moul* —4A **4**
Ashley Way. *North* —5A **10**
Ashpole Spinney. *North* —1D **18**
Ashridge Clo. *Rush* —5E **37**
Ash Ri. *North* —6B **2**
Ash St. *North* —2B **14**
Ashton Gro. *Well* —3F **27**
Ashtree Way. *North* —2D **12**
Ashwell Rd. *Rush* —3H **37**
Ashwood Rd. *North* —2D **12**
Askham Av. *Well* —4G **33**
Aspen Clo. *North* —4F **11**
Aspen Clo. *Rush* —2F **37**
Aster Clo. *North* —3H **15**
Aston Ri. *North* —1C **12**
Atterbury Way. *Gt Hou* —1C **22**
Attlee Clo. *North* —3G **9**
Attley Ct. *Well* —4G **33**
Auctioneers Ct. *North* —5C **14**
Auctioneers Way. *North* —5C **14**
Augusta Av. *North* —5A **20**
Austin Clo. *Irch* —5A **36**
Austin St. *North* —2C **14**
Austins Yd. *Earls B* —5A **32**
Avebury Way. *North* —3A **20**

Avenue Rd.—Buttermere Clo.

Avenue Rd. Well —6A 28
Avenue, The. Clif —4E 15
Avenue, The. Dal —2G 13
Avenue, The. Moul —5B 4
Avenue, The. North —1G 7
Avenue, The. Spin H —4F 9
Avenue, The. Well —5A 28
Aviemore Gdns. North —2F 19
Avignon Clo. New D —5B 6
Avon Clo. Well —5E 27
Avon Dri. North —6F 7
Axehead Rd. North —5G 13
Aynho Cres. North —2B 8
Aynho Wlk. North —2C 8
Azalea Clo. North —3A 16

Back La. Hard —3E 21
Badby Clo. North —3D 8
Badgers Wlk. North —2A 8
Bailey Ct. High F —6F 31
Bailiff St. North —2B 14
Baird Av. Upton —5E 13
Baird Ct. Park F —5D 26
Baker Cres. Irch —5G 35
Baker Ri. North —2B 8
Baker St. Irth —2C 30
Baker St. North —1B 14
Baker St. Well —6A 28
Bakewell Clo. North —3G 19
Baldwin Clo. North —3G 9
Balfour Rd. North —6B 8
Balham Clo. Rush —5D 36
Balland Way. Woot —4E 21
Ballantyne. Rush —4E 37
Balmoral Av. Rush —2G 37
Balmoral Clo. Earls B —6B 32
Balmoral Clo. Well —4G 33
Balmoral Rd. North —6B 8
Banbury Clo. North —1E 19
Banbury Clo. Well —4G 33
Banbury La. Roth & North —6A 18
Bankside. North —4E 9
Banks, The. Well —2H 27
Bank Vw. North —4A 20
Bants La. North —2E 13
(in two parts)
Baring Rd. North —2H 13
Barker Clo. Rush —3F 37
Barker Rd. Earls B —6A 32
Barley Hill Rd. North —6C 4
(in two parts)
Barley La. North —2A 8
Barlow La. Moul —4H 3
Barnard Clo. North —1C 12
Barn Corner. Col —1F 25
Barnet Clo. North —1H 19
Barnet's Stile. North —4B 8
Barnfield Clo. North —3A 8
Barnhill Sq. North —1D 10
Barn La. Mil M —2C 24
Barn M. Col —1F 25
Barn Owl Clo. North —3H 19
Barnstaple Clo. North —2B 16
Barn Way. Lodge F —4C 6
Barnwell Dri. Rush —5E 37
Barnwell Gdns. Well —4F 27
Barnwell Rd. North —3C 8
Barnwell Rd. Well —4F 27
Baron Av. Earls B —4B 32
Baronson Gdns. North —1E 15
Barons Way. North —3H 7
Barrack Rd. North —2B 14
Barret Clo. Well —1E 33
Barrett Clo. High F —6F 31
Barringers Ct. Irch —4H 35
Barringers Gdns. Irch —4H 35
Barrington Rd. Rush —5G 37
Barry Rd. North —2F 15
Bartons Clo., The. North —6G 7
Barwick Ho. Rush —3E 37
Basil Clo. North —5C 20
Bassett's Ct. Well —1H 33
Bates Clo. High F —6F 31
Baukewell Ct. North —4B 10
Baunhill Clo. North —2A 16
Baxter Ct. Hard —3E 21
Beacon Ct. North —6F 13
Beaconsfield Pl. Rush —2F 37
Beaconsfield Ter. North —2C 14
Beaconsfield Ter. Rush —2F 37
Beaufort Dri. North —6D 6
Beaumaris Clo. Rush —4G 37
Beaumont Ct. North —3B 14
(off Simon's Wlk.)
Beaumont Dri. North —4E 11
Beaune Clo. North —6A 6
Beauvais Ct. North —5A 6
Beck Ct. Well —5F 27
Becket Way. North —2G 9
Bective Rd. North —4B 8
Bedale Rd. Well —5A 28
Beddoes Clo. Woot —5E 21
Bede Clo. High F —6G 31
Bedford Mans. North —4C 14
(off Derngate)
Bedford Pl. North —4C 14
Bedford Rd. North & L Hou —4D 14
Bedford Rd. Rush —4G 37
Beech Av. North —5F 9
Beech Cres. Irch —6G 35
Beechcroft Gdns. North —5F 9
Beech Dri. Well —6G 27
Beech Gro. North —2A 10
Beech Rd. Rush —1F 37
Beechwood Dri. North —6B 10
Beechwood Rd. North —2D 12
Beeston Av. North —1C 16
Belfield Clo. North —4G 9
Belfry La. Col —6A 20
Bell Ct. Well —6A 28
(off Bell St.)
Bellropes Sq. North —5G 11
Bell St. Well —6A 28
Belstead Rd. North —3A 16
Belton Clo. North —3B 20
Belvedere Clo. North —2G 13
Belvoir Clo. North —6C 6
Belvoir Clo. Rush —5G 37
Bembridge Dri. North —6A 8
Benedict Clo. Rush —5D 36
Bengeworth Ct. Well —6A 28
Benham Ct. North —4C 10
Benjamin Sq. North —1G 19
Bentley Clo. North —3G 11
Bentley Ct. Fin R —2B 28
Bergerac Clo. New D —5A 6
Berkeley Clo. North —3E 15
Berkeley Houses. North —3B 14
(off Horsemarket)
Bern Links. North —6H 13
Bern Side. North —6H 13
Berrill St. Irch —6G 35
Berry Clo. Earls B —4A 32
Berry Clo. Roth —5C 18
Berrydale. North —4G 11
Berry La. Woot —6C 20
Berrymoor Ct. Well —3G 33
Berrymoor Rd. Well —4G 33
Berrywood Rd. North —1A 12
Bertrum Clo. North —6B 10
Berwick Ho. North —2C 8
Bestwell Ct. North —1D 16
Betony Wlk. Rush —5F 37
Bevan Clo. Fin R —4C 28
Beverley Cres. North —6G 9
Bewick Rd. North —2B 16
Bibury Clo. Well —4F 33
Bibury Cres. North —2A 10
Bidders Clo. North —5C 14
Bideford Clo. North —2A 16
Billing Brook Rd. North —2A 10
Billing La. Over & North —5C 4
Billingmead Sq. North —6F 11
Billingmead Wlk. Gt Bil —5E 11
(nr. Manor Farm Rd.)
Billingmead Wlk. North —6F 11
(nr. Gibbsacre Ct.)
Billing Rd. Braf G —3G 17
Billing Rd. North —3D 14
Billing Rd. E. North —3G 15
Billington St. North —2E 15
Bilsdon Clo. Rush —5D 36
Bilton Ct. Well —6F 27
Birchall Rd. Rush —3D 36
Birch Barn La. North —2H 7
Birch Barn Way. North —2A 8
Birchfield Ct. North —6G 9
Birchfield Cres. North —5H 9
Birchfield Rd. North —1E 15
Birchfield Rd. Well —1F 33
Birchfield Rd. E. North —6F 9
Birch Rd. Rush —3G 37
Birds Hill Rd. North —4C 10
Birds Hill Wlk. North —5C 10
(in two parts)
Birkdale Clo. North —4E 9
Bishops Dri. North —4A 8
Bitten Ct. North —4B 10
Blackberry La. North —6G 13
Blackfriars. Rush —4D 36
Black Lion Hill. North —4A 14
Blackthorn Bri. Ct. North —3E 11
Blackthorn Rd. North —3E 11
Blackthorn Wlk. North —4E 11
(in two parts)
Blackwell Hill. North —3G 19
Blackymore La. Woot —6C 20
Bladon Clo. North —2H 9
Blakesley Clo. North —2B 8
Blake Wlk. High F —6E 31
Blaydon Wlk. Well —4G 27
Bledlow Ri. North —3G 19
Blenheim Clo. Rush —4E 37
Blenheim Rd. North —1A 20
Blenheim Rd. Well —4F 27
Blinco Rd. Rush —3G 37
Blisworth & Milton Malsor By-Pass. Roth & North —6D 18
Bloomfield Clo. Rush —3E 37
Blossac Ct. North —6A 6
Blossom Way. L Bil —6D 10
Bluebell Ct. North —3H 15
Blue Bell Pk. Moul —4H 3
Bluebell Ri. Rush —5G 37
Blueberry Ri. North —5F 11
Bly La. North —4C 12
Boarden Clo. Moul I —6F 3
Board St. Irth —1D 30
Bobtail Ct. North —6D 6
Bollinger Clo. North —6A 6
Bondfield Av. North —4C 8
Booth Dri. Park F —1C 32
Booth La. N. North —2H 9
Booth La. S. North —4A 10
Booth Mdw. Ct. North —2B 10
Booth Mdw. Wlk. North —2A 10
Booth Ri. North —2H 9
(in two parts)
Bordeaux Clo. North —6A 6
Borough Ct. High F —6F 31
Borrowdale Wlk. North —3H 9
Bostock Av. North —2E 15
Bosworth Clo. North —2H 19
Botmead Rd. North —3F 11
Bouganvillea Dri. North —3H 15
Boughton Dri. Rush —5D 36
Boughton Fair La. Moul —2G 3
Boughton Grn. Rd. North & Moul P —3B 8
Boughton La. Moul —6E 3
Boughton Rd. Moul —5E 3
Boundary Av. Rush —3C 36
Bourne Clo. Well —5E 27
Bourne Cres. North —6F 7
Bourton Clo. North —3G 19
Bourton Way. Well —5G 33
Bouverie Rd. Hard —3E 21
Bouverie St. North —3E 15
Bouverie Wlk. North —3E 15
Bow Ct. North —6F 13
Bowden Rd. North —3H 13
Bower Wlk. North —1B 10
(in three parts)
Bowlers Yd. Earls B —5A 32
Bowmans Clo. North —2E 19
Bowness. Well —6E 27
Bowthorpe Clo. North —3A 16
Brackenfield Sq. North —6C 4
Brackenhill Clo. North —4D 8
Brackley Clo. North —1C 8
Brackmills Bus. Pk. North —1F 21
Bracknell. Well —1E 33
Bradden Clo. North —2C 8
Bradfield Clo. Fin R —2A 28
Bradfield Clo. Rush —2H 37
Bradfield Rd. Fin R —2A 28
Bradmoor Ct. North —2E 11
Bradshaw St. North —3B 14
Bradshaw Way. Irch —5F 35
Braemar Cres. North —3A 20
Brafield Rd. Cog —5G 17
Braid Ct. Well —4F 27
Bramble End. North —3G 19
Bramcote Dri. North —1C 16
Bramhall Ri. North —1C 12
Bramley Clo. Cog —3H 17
Bramley Clo. Rush —2D 36
Bramley Gro. North —5E 11
Brammar Ho. North —2G 13
Brampton Clo. Well —4F 27
Brampton La. Chap B —2A 2
Brampton Wlk. North —2E 9
Brancutt Ct. North —6E 11
Brancutt Wlk. North —5E 11
Branksome Av. North —6A 8
Brashland Dri. North —5C 20
Brawn Clo. Irth —3C 30
Brayford Clo. North —2H 15
Brecon St. North —1H 13
Breezehill. Woot —5E 21
Breezehill Way. Well —4A 28
Brembridge Clo. Syw —3G 5
Brendon Clo. North —2H 15
Brentford. Well —6D 26
Bressingham Gdns. North —4B 20
Bretton Clo. North —6B 6
Briar Hill Rd. North —1A 20
Briar Hill Wlk. North —1A 20
Briars, The. North —6H 13
Brickhill Rd. Well —1E 33
Brick Kiln La. North —1B 14
Brickwell Ct. North —6D 10
Brickyard. North —1G 9
Bridge St. North —4B 14
Bridgewater Dri. North —2H 15
Bridle Clo. Braf G —1G 23
Bridle Clo. Fin R —2A 28
Bridle Path. Braf G —1G 23
Brightwell Wlk. Irth —3B 30
Britannia Gdns. Well —1C 34
Briton Gdns. North —6G 9
Briton Rd. North —1G 15
Briton Ter. North —6G 9
Brittons Dri. North —6C 4
Broad Grn. Well —6H 27
Broadhurst Dri. North —1D 16
Broadlands. Pits —1C 2
Broadlands. Rush —2F 37
Broadmead Av. North —5F 9
Broad St. Earls B —5A 32
Broad St. North —3B 14
Broadway. North —6E 9
Broadway. Well —2A 34
Broadway E. North —6F 9
Brocade Clo. North —1G 19
Brockhall Clo. North —3D 8
Brockhall Rd. North —3D 8
Brockton St. North —6C 8
Brockwood Clo. North —6B 6
Bromford Clo. L Bil —1D 16
Brooke Clo. Rush —4F 37
Brooke Clo. Well —6D 26
Brooke Grn. Well —6D 26
Brooke M. Well —6D 26
Brookfield Rd. North —5D 8
Brookfield Rd. Rush —3E 37
Brookland Cres. North —6F 9
Brookland Rd. North —6E 9
Brook La. North —1G 13
Brookside Meadows. North —6F 7
Brook St. North —2A 14
Brook St. E. Well —1B 34
Brook St. W. Well —1H 33
Brook Ter. Irth —1B 30
Brook Va. Wilby —4E 33
Broom Ct. North —6G 13
Broomhill Cres. North —1D 10
Brough Clo. North —6A 6
Broughton Pl. North —4G 9
Browning Rd. Well —1E 33
Brownlow Ct. North —3B 10
Browns Clo. Moul —3H 3
Browns Way. North —4D 14
Bruce St. North —3G 13
Brundall Clo. North —2A 16
Brunel Clo. Park F —5D 26
Brunel Dri. Upton —4D 12
Brunswick Pl. North —2D 14
Brunswick Wlk. North —2D 14
(off Brunswick Pl.)
Brunting Rd. Moul —5H 3
Bryant Way. High F —5F 31
Buchanan Clo. North —6H 13
Buckingham Clo. North —4A 20
Buckingham Clo. Well —4G 33
Buckwell Clo. Well —6G 27
Buckwell End. Well —6H 27
Buckwell Pl. Well —1H 33
Bullfinch Way. Well —5B 28
Bunting Rd. North —6B 8
Bunting Rd. Ind. Est. North —6C 8
Burford Av. North —2A 10
Burford Way. Well —3F 33
Burleigh Rd. North —6B 8
Burmans Way. Cog —3H 17
Burns Clo. Earls B —5B 32
Burns Rd. Well —1D 32
Burns St. North —2D 14
Burrows Ct. North —3B 10
Burryport Rd. Brac I —1G 21
Burton Ct. North —3H 9
Burwood Rd. North —5G 9
Bury Clo. High F —5G 31
Burystead Pl. Well —1A 34
Bush Clo. Well —6G 27
Bush Hill. North —6H 9
Bushland Rd. North —5H 9
Butcher's La. Bou —5B 2
Butlin Ct. Well —4C 34
Buttermere. Well —6E 27
Buttermere Clo. North —4H 9

A-Z Northampton 39

Buttmead. *Blis* —6A **24**
Butts Cft. Clo. *North* —5B **20**
Butts Rd. *North* —5B **20**
Butts Rd. *Well* —4G **33**
Byfield Rd. *North* —3H **13**
Byron Cres. *High F* —6E **31**
Byron Cres. *North* —3C **36**
Byron Rd. *Well* —1F **33**
Byron St. *North* —6E **9**

Caldbeck Wlk. *North* —3H **9**
Calder Grn. *North* —6F **7**
(in two parts)
Calstock Clo. *North* —2A **16**
Camberley Clo. *North* —5E **11**
Camborne Clo. *North* —2A **20**
Cambria Cres. *North* —6H **9**
Cambridge St. *North* —1B **14**
Cambridge St. *Well* —6A **28**
Camelot Way. *North* —1B **12**
Cameron Clo. *North* —2F **13**
Cameron Cres. *North* —2F **13**
Cameron Dri. *North* —2F **13**
Campanula Clo. *North* —3H **15**
Campbell Rd. *Well* —3A **34**
Campbell Sq. *Earls B* —5A **32**
Campbell Sq. *North* —3B **14**
Campbell St. *North* —2B **14**
Campion Clo. *Rush* —5F **37**
Campion Ct. *North* —6E **11**
Camp La. *North* —6A **12**
Camrose Rd. *North* —1H **13**
Candace Ct. *North* —1F **13**
Candleford. *North* —3B **8**
Cannon St. *Well* —6A **28**
Canonby. *Well* —1E **33**
Canons Wlk. *North* —4H **7**
Cardigan Clo. *North* —1G **13**
Cardinal Clo. *North* —4A **20**
Cares Orchard. *Braf G* —6G **17**
Carey Clo. *Moul* —4G **3**
Carey St. *North* —2D **14**
Carey Way. *Rush* —2H **37**
Carline Ct. *North* —3A **10**
Carlton Clo. *Rush* —6E **37**
Carlton Gdns. *North* —6D **8**
Carlton M. *High F* —6G **31**
Carlton Rd. *North* —5D **8**
Carlyle Av. *North* —2F **13**
Carmarthen Way. *Rush* —5G **37**
Carnegie St. *Rush* —3E **37**
Carousel Way. *North* —2C **16**
Carrington Gdns. *North* —1C **16**
Carter Clo. *Well* —1B **34**
Cartmel Pl. *North* —4G **9**
Cartmel Way. *Rush* —2H **37**
Cartwright Rd. *North* —6B **8**
Casterbridge Ct. *Hard* —4D **20**
Casterton Wlk. *North* —2F **11**
Castilian St. *North* —4C **14**
Castilian Ter. *North* —4C **14**
Castle Av. *North* —1D **12**
Castle Bush. *North* —1D **12**
Castle Clo. *North* —1D **12**
Castle Ct. *Rush* —5E **37**
Castle Hill. *North* —3A **14**
Castle La. *Well* —1A **34**
Castle M. *Well* —1B **34**
Castle Rd. *Well* —1B **34**
Castle St. *North* —3B **14**
Castle St. *Well* —1B **34**
Castle Ter. *North* —3A **14**
Castle Way. *Well* —1A **34**
Caswell Rd. *Brac I* —2F **21**
Catesby Clo. *North* —3D **8**
Cattle Hill. *Gt Bil* —5F **11**
Cattle Mkt. Rd. *North* —4B **14**
Catton Cres. *North* —2G **7**
Cauldecott Clo. *North* —2D **18**
Causeway, The. *Gt Bil & Cog* —2F **17**
Causeway, The. *North* —6G **13**
Cavendish Dri. *North* —3A **16**
Cecil Rd. *North* —6B **8**
Cedar Clo. *Irch* —6G **35**
Cedar Clo. *Rush* —5E **37**
Cedar Clo. *Syw* —6G **5**
Cedar Ct. *North* —1F **13**
Cedar Rd. *North* —1E **15**
Cedar Rd. E. *North* —6F **9**
Cedar Way. *High F* —4F **31**
Cedarway. *North* —4H **27**
Cedrus Ct. *North* —1G **7**
Celeborn Pl. *North* —2E **11**
Cemetery La. *High F* —5F **31**
Centaine. *Rush* —4E **37**
Central Av. *North* —1A **8**
Central Av. *North* —3G **33**

Chace Rd. *Well* —1C **34**
Chadstone Av. *North* —1C **8**
Chadwick Gdns. *North* —6E **7**
Chaffinch Clo. *North* —4G **19**
Chalcombe Av. *North* —2B **8**
Chalcombe Rd. *North* —3B **8**
Chalk La. *North* —4A **14**
Chamberlain Av. *Well* —4G **33**
Chamberlain Way. *High F* —6G **31**
Chantry Clo. *Gt Bil* —4E **11**
Chapel Grn. *North* —5H **7**
Chapel Hill. *High F* —3F **31**
Chapel Hill. *Irch* —5H **35**
Chapel La. *Blis* —5A **24**
Chapel La. *Braf G* —1H **23**
Chapel La. *Gt Dod* —6G **33**
Chapel Pl. *North* —3D **14**
Chapel Row. *Gt Bil* —5F **11**
(off Station M.)
Chapmans Clo. *Irch* —5H **35**
Chappell Ho. *North* —5H **3**
Chardonnay Clo. *New D* —5B **6**
Charlbury Clo. *Well* —5G **33**
Charles Clo. *High F* —4G **31**
Charles Partridge Ct. *Well* —4E **33**
Charles Robinson Ct. *Well* —2G **33**
Charles St. *North* —2C **14**
Charles St. *Well* —3G **33**
Charlton Clo. *North* —2B **8**
Charnwood Av. *North* —5A **10**
Chartwell Av. *North* —2H **9**
Chase, The. *Pit* —1C **2**
Chater St. *Moul* —4A **4**
Chatsworth Av. *North* —2C **10**
Chatsworth Dri. *Well* —4E **27**
Chaucer Rd. *North* —1E **33**
Chaucer St. *North* —5E **9**
Cheddar Clo. *North* —2E **13**
Chedworth Clo. *North* —5G **11**
Cheese La. *Well* —1A **34**
(off Market St.)
Chelfham Clo. *North* —2A **16**
Chelmsford Clo. *North* —1H **19**
Chelveston Rd. *High F* —5H **31**
Chepstow Clo. *North* —2H **13**
Chepstow Dri. *Well* —4E **27**
Chequers La. *Well* —6A **28**
Cheriton Way. *North* —3H **15**
Cherry Av. *Well* —4A **28**
Cherry Blossom Clo. *North* —5E **11**
Cherry Clo. *North* —5H **9**
Cherry Ct. *Irch* —2C **30**
Cherry Lodge Rd. *North* —3E **11**
Cherry Orchard. *Rush* —4G **37**
Cherry St. *Irch* —2C **30**
Cherry Tree La. *Gt Hou* —6B **16**
Cherrytree Wlk. *Syw* —5G **5**
Cherwell Grn. *North* —6G **7**
Chesham Ri. *North* —3E **11**
Chester Av. *Irch* —3G **35**
Chester Rd. *Rush* —3D **36**
Chester Rd. *Well* —1C **34**
Chestnut Av. *Woot* —6C **20**
Chestnut Clo. *Rush* —2D **36**
Chestnut Rd. *North* —6F **9**
Chestnut Ter. *North* —5F **9**
Cheviot Ct. *North* —6F **13**
Chewton Clo. *North* —2E **13**
Cheyne Wlk. *North* —4C **14**
Chichele Clo. *High F* —6F **31**
(off Hind Stile)
Chichele St. *High F* —5G **31**
Chieftan Bus. Pk. *Well* —5C **26**
Chiltern Av. *North* —1E **13**
Chiltern Clo. *North* —1E **13**
Chiltern Way. *North* —1E **13**
Chilwell Ct. *North* —1C **16**
Chipsey Av. *North* —3G **15**
Choakles, The. *Woot* —5G **21**
Chowns Mill Bus. Pk. *High F* —3F **31**
Christchurch Av. *North* —2C **34**
Christchurch Rd. *North* —2F **15**
Chulmleigh Wlk. *North* —2H **15**
(in two parts)
Church Clo. *Mil M* —1C **24**
Churchfield Clo. *North* —3D **8**
Church Grn. *North* —5G **7**
(in two parts)
Church Hill. *Rush* —4D **36**
Church Hill. *Moul* —4H **3**
Church Hill. *Woot* —6D **20**
Churchill Av. *North* —3G **9**
Churchill Av. *Well* —4G **33**
Churchill Rd. *Earls B* —5A **32**
Church La. *Blis* —6A **24**
Church La. *Braf G* —1H **23**
Church La. *Gt Dod* —6G **33**
Church La. *Harl* —1A **6**

Church La. *L Bil* —1D **16**
Church La. *North* —3B **14**
Church La. *Pit* —1C **2**
Church La. *Syw* —2G **5**
Church La. *Wilby* —4D **32**
Church St. *Bou* —5B **2**
Church St. *Irth* —1D **30**
Church St. *Moul* —4H **3**
Church St. *Roth* —5B **18**
Church St. *Rush* —3F **37**
Church St. *Well* —1A **34**
Church Vw. *Moul* —3H **3**
Church Vw. *North* —4A **8**
Church Vw. *Woot* —6D **20**
Church Wlk. *Gt Bil* —5E **11**
Church Wlk. *Irth* —1D **30**
(off Church St.)
Churchway. *North* —6C **14**
Church Way. *Well* —1A **34**
(off Orient Way)
Church Way Ct. *North* —1A **16**
Cinnamon Clo. *North* —5C **20**
Circus End. *North* —6D **6**
Cissbury Rd. *North* —5G **13**
Clannell Rd. *North* —3H **19**
Clare Clo. *Earls B* —6B **32**
Claregate. *North* —3A **20**
Claremont Ct. *North* —3B **14**
(off Simon's Wlk.)
Clarence Av. *North* —6B **8**
Clarence Ct. *Rush* —5E **37**
Clare Rd. *Well* —2E **33**
Clare St. *North* —2C **14**
Clare Wlk. *High F* —6F **31**
Clarke Ct. *Earls B* —5B **32**
Clarke Rd. *North* —1F **15**
Claughton Rd. *North* —6C **14**
Claydon Clo. *Well* —6G **27**
Clayfield Clo. *Moul I* —1G **9**
Claystones. *North* —1E **19**
Clee Ri. *North* —1E **13**
Cleeve Way. *Well* —4F **33**
Cleveland Pl. *North* —1H **19**
Cliftonville. *North* —3D **14**
Cliftonville Ct. *North* —3E **15**
Cliftonville Rd. *North* —3E **15**
Clinton Rd. *North* —6A **14**
Clipston Pl. *North* —5F **11**
Clipston Way. *North* —6D **6**
Clock Tower Ct. *North* —1B **10**
Close, The. *Irth* —2D **30**
Close, The. *North* —3B **8**
Cloutsham St. *North* —2C **14**
Clover Dri. *Rush* —5G **37**
Clover La. *North* —2H **7**
Clumber Dri. *North* —2B **16**
Coaching Wlk. *North* —5A **10**
Cobblestone Ct. *North* —1E **19**
Cob Dri. *Swan V* —2C **18**
Codlin Clo. *L Bil* —6D **10**
Coffee Tavern Clo. *North* —3F **37**
(off High St.)
Coffee Tavern La. *Rush* —3F **37**
Coldstream La. *Hard* —3D **20**
Coleraine Clo. *North* —3H **7**
College Fld. Clo. *North* —4F **11**
College St. *High F* —5G **31**
College St. *Irth* —1C **30**
College St. *North* —3B **14**
College St. *Rush* —3F **37**
College St. *Well* —1G **33**
Collingcroft Clo. *North* —4H **19**
Collingdale Rd. *North* —4A **10**
Collingtree Rd. *Mil M* —1C **24**
Collingwood Rd. *North* —6E **9**
Collins St. *North* —2E **15**
Collmead Ct. *North* —3E **11**
Collyweston Rd. *North* —2F **11**
Colne Way. *North* —6F **7**
Colonial Dri. *North* —6B **20**
Colwell Rd. *Well* —1C **34**
Colwyn Rd. *North* —2D **14**
Commercial St. *High F* —6F **31**
Commercial St. *North* —4B **14**
Commercial Way. *Well* —1A **34**
Compton Clo. *Earls B* —6A **32**
Compton Rd. *Well* —6C **28**
Compton St. *North* —3B **14**
Compton Way. *Earls B* —6A **32**
Conduit La. *North* —3B **14**
Coneygree Clo. *North* —6E **11**
Coneygreen. *North* —3E **21**
Coneygree Wlk. *North* —6E **11**
Coneywell Ct. *North* —6C **10**
Conifer Ri. *North* —6B **10**
Coniston Av. *North* —4G **9**
Coniston Clo. *Well* —6E **27**
Connaught St. *North* —2C **14**

Connegar Leys. *Blis* —6B **24**
Constable Rd. *North* —4B **10**
Conway Clo. *North* —5F **7**
Conway Clo. *Rush* —5E **37**
Conway Clo. *Well* —5E **27**
Conyngham Rd. *North* —5C **10**
Cook Pl. *North* —5G **11**
Co-operative Row. *Rush* —4F **37**
Copper Leaf Clo. *Moul* —1H **9**
Coppice Dri. *North* —2F **9**
Copse Clo. *North* —2G **7**
Copymoor Clo. *Woot* —5E **21**
Corbieres Clo. *New D* —5B **6**
Cordon Clo. *North* —4E **11**
Cordon Cres. *Earls B* —5B **32**
Cordwainers. *Rush* —4G **37**
Cornfield Clo. *North* —2A **8**
Cornhill Clo. *Lodge F* —4D **6**
Corn Kiln Clo. *Cog* —3H **17**
Corn La. *Well* —1A **34**
Cornwall Bus. Pk. *North* —1G **21**
Coronation Av. *Rush* —4C **36**
Corran Clo. *North* —1F **13**
Cosgrove Rd. *North* —2B **8**
Cosgrove Way. *North* —2B **8**
Cotswold Av. *North* —1D **12**
Cotswold Dri. *Well* —4F **33**
Cotswold Ho. *North* —1D **12**
Cottage Clo. *North* —3H **7**
Cottage Gdns. *North* —4E **11**
Cottagewell Ct. *North* —6C **10**
Cottarville. *North* —6A **10**
Cottesbrooke Gdns. *North* —4C **20**
Cottesmore Clo. *North* —6C **6**
Cottesmore Way. *Well* —1F **33**
Cottingham Dri. *Moul* —6G **3**
Cotton End. *North* —5B **14**
Cottons, The. *Well* —4F **27**
Coulon Clo. *Irch* —6G **35**
Countess Ct. *North* —2H **13**
Countess Rd. *North* —2H **13**
Courteen Hall Clo. *North* —2C **8**
Courteenhall Rd. *Blis* —5A **24**
Courteney. *Rush* —4E **37**
Court Rd. *North* —4B **14**
Coverack Clo. *North* —2A **20**
Coverdale. *North* —2G **7**
Covert Clo. *North* —1H **7**
Covington St. *North* —3F **15**
Cowgill Clo. *North* —4E **11**
Cowley Clo. *Woot* —4C **20**
Cowper Clo. *Earls B* —5C **32**
Cowper Clo. *Irth* —2B **30**
Cowper Rd. *Well* —1E **33**
Cowper St. *North* —2D **14**
Cowper Ter. *North* —6D **8**
Cowslip Clo. *Rush* —5G **37**
Cow Yd. *North* —4A **8**
Crabb St. *Rush* —4F **37**
Crabb Tree Dri. *North* —6C **4**
Crabtree Clo. *Well* —3H **33**
Cracknuts La. *Gt Hou* —1B **22**
Cragside. *Well* —6G **27**
Craigie. *Well* —1E **33**
Cranbrook Rd. *North* —6B **8**
Crane Clo. *Den I* —3A **34**
Crane Wlk. *North* —1B **10**
Cranford Rd. *North* —4B **8**
Cranmere Av. *North* —3G **15**
Cransley Wlk. *North* —1F **11**
(in two parts)
Cranstoun St. *North* —2C **14**
Craven St. *North* —2C **14**
Crawford Av. *North* —2F **13**
Crawley Av. *Well* —4F **27**
Crediton Clo. *North* —2A **16**
Crescent, The. *Moul* —4A **4**
Crescent, The. *North* —1E **15**
Crescent, The. *Rush* —3C **36**
Cresswell Rd. *Rush* —3D **36**
Crestline Ct. *North* —2D **10**
Crestwood Gdns. *North* —2C **10**
Crestwood Rd. *North* —1B **10**
Cricklade Clo. *North* —3A **16**
Crickly Cres. *North* —6F **13**
Crispian Ct. *North* —3E **37**
Crispin St. *North* —3B **14**
Crocket Clo. *North* —5D **8**
Crocus Way. *Rush* —6F **37**
Croft Clo. *Well* —6E **27**
Crofters Clo. *North* —4A **20**
Croftmeadow Ct. *North* —3E **11**
Croft, The. *North* —6G **7**
Croft Way. *Rush* —2H **37**
Cromwell Ct. *Well* —6B **28**
Cromwell Rd. *Rush* —2G **37**
Cromwell St. *North* —3B **14**
Crossbrooks. *Woot* —5E **21**

Cross Rd. *Well* —5B **28**
Cross St. *Moul* —4H **3**
Cross, The. *Gt Hou* —1B **22**
Cross Waters Clo. *Woot* —5E **21**
Cross Way. *Irth* —3B **30**
Crouch Way. *Irth* —2D **30**
Croughton Clo. *North* —2B **8**
Crowberry Av. *Moul* —6H **3**
Crow La. *L Bil* —1F **17**
Crow La. Ind. Est. *North* —1F **17**
Crownsmead. *North* —2E **19**
Crown Way. *Rush* —1C **36**
Crowthorp Rd. *North* —2F **11**
Croxdale Clo. *North* —2G **7**
Croyland Rd. *Well* —1G **33**
Cubleigh Clo. *Moul* —1F **19**
Cullahill Ct. *North* —1F **19**
Culworth Cres. *North* —2C **8**
Cumberland Clo. *North* —4F **9**
Cumbrae Dri. *Gt Hou* —5F **11**
Cunningham Clo. *High F* —6F **31**
Curlbrook Clo. *Woot* —4E **21**
Currie Rd. *North* —6B **8**
· Curtis M. *Well* —4E **27**
Curtlee Hill. *North* —5E **21**
Cyclamen Way. *North* —3H **15**
Cypress Ct. *North* —4B **10**
Cyril St. *North* —3D **14**

Daffodil Dri. *Rush* —6F **37**
Daimler Clo. *North* —3G **11**
Dairymeadow Ct. *North* —1C **10**
Daisy Cft. *Rush* —5G **37**
Dale Av. *Well* —6E **27**
Dale Clo. *Well* —6E **27**
Dale Ho. *Well* —1H **33**
(off Wood St.)
Dalestones. *North* —1E **19**
Dale St. *Well* —1H **33**
Dale, The. *Well* —6E **27**
Dalkeith Rd. *Well* —4H **33**
Dallington Ct. *North* —1G **13**
Dallington Grn. *North* —1G **13**
Dallington Haven. *North* —1G **13**
Dallington Pk. Rd. *North* —1G **13**
Dallington Rd. *North* —1G **13**
Dalston Wlk. *North* —3H **9**
Damson Dell. *L Bil* —1D **16**
Danefield Rd. *North* —5G **9**
Dane Ridge. *North* —3D **12**
Danes Backside. *North* —4A **8**
Danes Camp Way. *North* —1E **19**
Danetree Gdns. *North* —5G **9**
Danewood Gdns. *North* —5G **9**
Daniels Rd. *L Irch* —4C **34**
Dapplestone Clo. *North* —1E **19**
Darby Clo. *Park F* —6C **26**
Dark La. *Gt Har* —1F **27**
Darwin Wlk. *North* —6D **6**
(in two parts)
Da Vinci Clo. *Upton* —4D **12**
Davy Clo. *Park F* —5C **26**
Dayrell Rd. *North* —1F **19**
Dayrell Sq. *North* —1G **19**
Dayrell Wlk. *North* —1G **19**
Dayton St. *Rush* —3E **37**
Deacon Clo. *Rush* —2H **37**
Deacons Ct. *North* —3F **11**
Deal Ct. *North* —2C **14**
Deal St. *North* —2B **14**
Dean Clo. *Rush* —5E **37**
Deancourt Dri. *North* —6B **6**
Deansway. *North* —3F **11**
Debdale Rd. *North* —4H **9**
Debdale Rd. *Well* —6G **27**
Deer Pk. Rd. *Moul I* —1F **9**
Delamere Rd. *North* —2B **20**
Delapre Ct. *North* —1B **20**
Delapre Cres. *North* —6B **14**
Delapre Cres. Rd. *North* —6A **14**
Delapre St. *North* —6A **14**
Dell Cres. *North* —2E **11**
Dell Pl. *Rush* —3G **37**
Delta Way. *North* —2G **7**
Denbigh Rd. *North* —3A **16**
Denby Dale. *Well* —4F **27**
Dencora Bus. Pk. *Well* —1C **32**
Dene Clo. *Well* —5F **27**
Denford Way. *Well* —4F **27**
Denington Ct. *Den I* —3A **34**
Denington Ind. Est. *Well* —3B **34**
Denington Rd. *Den I* —3A **34**
Denmark Ct. *Rush* —4G **37**
Denmark Rd. *North* —3D **14**
Denmark Rd. *Rush* —4G **37**
Denston Clo. *Irch* —5H **35**
Denton Clo. *Irch* —5H **35**

Denton Clo. *Rush* —2G **37**
Derby Rd. *North* —2D **14**
Derngate. *North* —4C **14**
Derwent Clo. *North* —5G **7**
Derwent Clo. *Well* —5E **27**
Derwent Dri. *North* —6G **7**
Devonshire Clo. *Bou* —5B **2**
Devonshire Rd. *North* —5G **27**
Devon Wlk. *Rush* —4G **37**
Devon Way. *North* —2F **9**
Diamond Dri. *Irth* —3B **30**
Diamond Way. *North* —1E **31**
Dianan Ho. *Well* —6F **27**
Dickson Clo. *North* —6G **13**
Dimock Sq. *North* —1G **19**
Dingle Rd. *Rush* —3B **36**
Dingley Wlk. *North* —2F **11**
Ditchford Clo. *Woot* —5E **21**
Ditchford Rd. *Well* —4H **29**
Dobson Clo. *North* —1C **22**
Doctors La. *Gt Dod* —6G **33**
Doddington Rd. *Earls B* —5B **32**
Doddington Rd. *Well* —5H **33**
Doddington Rd. *Wilby* —5D **32**
Doddridge St. *North* —4B **14**
Donellan Grn. *North* —1C **10**
Donovan Ct. *North* —1B **16**
Dorchester Ct. *North* —5B **6**
Dore Clo. *North* —2E **11**
Dorset Gdns. *North* —4C **8**
Dorset Rd. *North* —4C **8**
Douglas Rd. *North* —1A **12**
Dover Clo. *Rush* —4H **37**
Dove's La. *Moul* —4A **4**
Downs, The. *Well* —2C **27**
Downsway. *North* —5A **20**
Downthorpe Hill. *Earls B* —6A **32**
Downwood Clo. *North* —4F **11**
Dowthorpe End. *Earls B* —5A **32**
Drapery. *North* —3B **14**
Draycott Clo. *North* —2A **16**
Drayton Clo. *Rush* —5E **37**
Drayton Pl. *Irth* —1B **30**
Drayton Rd. *Irth* —1B **30**
Drayton Wlk. *North* —3C **8**
Drive, The. *Dus* —2B **12**
Drive, The. *North* —1E **15**
Drive, The. *Rush* —4F **37**
Drive, The. *Well* —2A **34**
Drovers Wlk. *North* —2H **7**
Druids Way. *North* —2E **9**
Drum La. *North* —3B **14**
Drummond Clo. *Pit* —1C **2**
Drydale Av. *North* —4G **9**
Dryden Rd. *North* —2G **13**
Dryden Rd. *Well* —6C **28**
Dryden Way. *High F* —6E **31**
Dryland Rd. *North* —5H **9**
Dryleys Ct. *North* —3E **14**
Drywell Ct. *North* —6D **10**
Duce Clo. *Well* —4F **27**
Duchy Clo. *High F* —6G **31**
Duck St. *Rush* —3F **37**
Duckworth Dell. *North* —1C **10**
Duke St. *North* —2C **14**
Duke St. *Well* —3F **33**
Dulce Rd. *North* —1D **12**
Dulley Av. *Well* —4H **33**
Dulverton Rd. *North* —2A **16**
Duncan Clo. *Moul P* —6E **3**
Duncan Ct. *Well* —3F **33**
Dundee St. *North* —3G **13**
Dunster St. *North* —3C **14**
Duston Mill La. *North* —4E **13**
Duston Rd. *North* —2E **13**
Duston Wildes. *North* —5B **6**
Dybdale Cres. *Well* —6G **27**
Dychurch La. *North* —3C **14**

Eagle Dri. *North* —1D **20**
Ealing Ter. *Rush* —2E **37**
Earlsfield Rd. *Woot* —5E **21**
Earl St. *North* —2C **14**
Eastbank. *North* —1B **10**
E. Butterfield Ct. *North* —2C **10**
East Cres. *Rush* —3D **36**
Eastern Av. N. *North* —2C **8**
Eastern Av. S. *North* —5C **8**
Eastern Clo. *North* —2C **8**
Eastfield. *Blis* —6A **24**
Eastfield Rd. *North* —6D **6**
Eastfield Rd. *Del* —6B **14**
Eastfield Rd. *Dus* —1C **12**
Eastfield Rd. *Irth* —1D **30**
Eastfield Rd. *Well* —5B **28**
East Gro. *Rush* —2F **37**
E. Leys Ct. *Moul* —6H **3**

E. Mead Ct. *North* —6D **10**
E. Oval. *North* —5G **7**
E. Paddock Ct. *North* —3D **10**
E. Park Pde. *North* —1E **15**
E. Priors Ct. *North* —3D **10**
E. Rising. *North* —4C **20**
East St. *Irch* —5H **35**
East St. *North* —3E **15**
Eaton Rd. *North* —6B **6**
Eaton Wlk. *Rush* —3F **37**
Ebbw Va. Rd. *Irth* —2B **30**
Ecton Brook Rd. *North* —4G **11**
Ecton La. *Syw* —2G **5**
Ecton Pk. Rd. *North* —4F **11**
Ecton St. *North* —3D **14**
Eden Clo. *North* —3G **9**
Edgehill Rd. *North* —6E **7**
Edgemead Clo. *Rou S* —6B **4**
Edgemont Rd. *North* —6B **10**
Edges Ct. *Moul* —6H **3**
Edinburgh Rd. *North* —5B **8**
Edinburgh Rd. *Well* —4G **33**
Edison Clo. *Park F* —5C **26**
Edison Ct. *Well* —6G **26**
Edison Dri. *Upton* —5E **13**
Edith St. *North* —3D **14**
Edmonds Clo. *Den I* —3A **34**
Edward Clo. *High F* —4G **31**
Edwardian Ct. *Woot* —4D **20**
Edward Rd. *Irch* —6H **35**
Edwards Dri. *Well* —6F **27**
Edward Watson Clo. *North* —2A **8**
Edwinstowe Clo. *North* —2B **16**
Ekins Clo. *North* —5A **10**
Eldean Rd. *North* —6C **6**
Elderberry Ct. *North* —4F **11**
Elgin St. *North* —3A **14**
Elizabeth Clo. *Earls B* —4A **32**
Elizabeth Clo. *Well* —3F **33**
Elizabeth Ct. *High F* —4G **31**
Elizabeth St. *North* —3E **15**
Elizabeth Wlk. *North* —3E **15**
Elizabeth Way. *Earls B* —4A **32**
Elizabeth Way. *High F* —3G **31**
Elizabeth Way. *Irth* —3C **30**
Ellan Clo. *Rush* —2C **36**
Ellesmere Av. *North* —2F **13**
Ellfield Ct. *North* —4C **10**
Elm Clo. *Braf G* —1G **23**
Elmhurst Av. *North* —5F **9**
Elmhurst St. *North* —5F **9**
Elmington Rd. *North* —2F **11**
Elm St. *North* —2C **14**
Elm St. *Well* —5H **27**
Elm Wlk. *High F* —5F **31**
Elmwood Wlk. *North* —6C **6**
Elsden Rd. *Well* —6C **28**
Elton Clo. *North* —4G **9**
Elwes Way. *Gt Bil* —5E **11**
Elysium Ter. *North* —1B **14**
Embankment, The. *Well* —3C **34**
Emerald Way. *North* —4A **14**
Emley Clo. *North* —6C **6**
Enfield Clo. *North* —1A **12**
Ennerdale Clo. *North* —4F **9**
Ennerdale Rd. *North* —4F **9**
Ennerdale Rd. *Rush* —2H **37**
Enstone Ct. *Well* —4G **33**
Enterprise Ct. *Well* —5D **26**
Entwood Dri. *North* —2E **11**
Ermine Rd. *North* —2F **11**
Esher Ct. *North* —3A **10**
Eskdale Av. *North* —4G **9**
Eskdale Clo. *Well* —4C **27**
Essex Rd. *Rush* —4G **37**
Essex St. *North* —1B **14**
Ethel St. *North* —3D **14**
Euston Rd. *North* —5B **14**
Evelyn Way. *Irch* —6A **36**
Evenley Rd. *North* —2B **8**
Evensford Wlk. *Irth* —3B **30**
Everdon Clo. *North* —3D **8**
Everitt Clo. *Den I* —3B **34**
Evesham Clo. *Well* —4G **33**
Evesham St. *North* —6D **4**
Excalibur Clo. *North* —2B **12**
Excelsior. *Well* —1D **32**
Excelsior Ct. *Irth* —1C **30**
Excelsior Gdns. *North* —1B **12**
Exeter Pl. *North* —2D **14**
Exmoor Clo. *North* —1E **15**
Express Clo. *Irch* —3C **30**
Express Pk. *Rush* —2B **36**
Eynon Clo. *Moul* —4G **3**

Fairfield Rd. *North* —5E **9**
Fairground Way. *Riv B* —3B **16**

Fairhurst Way. *Earls B* —5B **32**
Fairmead Cres. *Rush* —5D **36**
Fairmead Ri. *North* —1G **7**
Fair Mile. *North* —1H **7**
Fairoaks, The. *North* —1C **16**
Fairway. *North* —5D **8**
Fairway, The. *Well* —2G **27**
Falconers Ri. *North* —3H **19**
Falcutt Way. *North* —2C **8**
Fallowfield. *Well* —3G **27**
Fallow Wlk. *North* —1H **7**
Faracre Ct. *North* —6E **11**
Faracre Wlk. *North* —6E **11**
Faraday Clo. *Park F* —5C **26**
Faraday Clo. *Upton* —4E **13**
Faraday Ct. *Park F* —5C **26**
Faramir Pl. *North* —2E **11**
Faringdon Ct. *North* —6D **4**
Farmbrook Ct. *North* —2C **10**
Farm Clo. *North* —4A **8**
Farmclose Rd. *Woot* —5D **20**
Far Mdw. Ct. *North* —2B **10**
Farm Fld. Ct. *North* —2B **10**
Farmhill Rd. *North* —1H **7**
Farndish Rd. *Irch* —5H **35**
Farndon Clo. *North* —1H **7**
Farnham Dri. *Rush* —5D **36**
Farnworth Clo. *North* —6D **6**
Farraxton Sq. *North* —1F **19**
Favell Way. *North* —1A **16**
Fawsley Rd. *North* —1B **20**
Faxfield Wlk. *North* —6C **10**
Faxton Clo. *North* —3C **8**
Fellmead Rd. *North* —2F **11**
Fell Wlk. *Well* —5F **27**
Fengate Clo. *North* —2F **11**
Fennel Ct. *North* —6C **20**
Fenners Clo. *Rush* —3H **37**
Ferndale Rd. *North* —5A **10**
Fernie Fld. *Moul* —1H **9**
Fernie Way. *Well* —2G **27**
Fern Rd. *Rush* —3C **36**
Ferrers Ct. *High F* —4G **31**
Ferrestone Rd. *Well* —5A **28**
Ferris Row. *Riv B* —2C **16**
Fetter St. *North* —4C **14**
Fieldmill Rd. *North* —6E **11**
Fld. Nose Sq. *North* —5F **11**
Fields Vw. *Well* —1B **34**
Fieldway. *North* —6G **9**
Fienesgate. *North* —2E **19**
Fife St. *North* —2G **13**
Filleigh Way. *North* —2H **15**
Finedon Rd. *Irth* —1A **30**
Finedon Rd. *Well* —6B **28**
Finedon Rd. Ind. Est. *Well* —2B **28**
Firbank Clo. *North* —1C **16**
Firdale Av. *Rush* —1F **37**
Firs Ct. *Hard* —3E **21**
First Av. *Well* —2F **33**
Firsview Dri. *North* —6C **6**
Fir Tree Wlk. *North* —5B **10**
Fishers Clo. *North* —6E **11**
Fishponds Rd. *L Bil* —6D **10**
Fish St. *North* —3C **14**
Fitzroy Pl. *North* —3A **14**
Fitzroy Ter. *North* —2B **14**
Fitzwilliam Leys. *High F* —4F **31**
Fitzwilliam Rd. *Irth* —1B **30**
Fitzwilliam St. *Rush* —3E **37**
Five Acres Fold. *North* —6G **13**
Flaxlands Ct. *North* —4C **10**
Flaxwell Ct. *North* —1C **16**
Fleetwind Dri. *North* —4C **20**
Fleming Clo. *Park F* —4D **26**
Fletcher Rd. *Rush* —2E **37**
Flintcomb Ri. *North* —4E **11**
Flinters Clo. *Woot* —4E **21**
Florence Rd. *North* —2E **15**
Floribunda Dri. *North* —6G **13**
Ford La. *North* —6G **15**
Forest Ct. *Rush* —2H **37**
Forest Rd. *North* —6B **14**
Forfar St. *North* —2G **13**
Fort Pl. *North* —3A **14**
Fosberry Clo. *Woot* —5E **21**
Foskett Ct. *North* —2E **37**
Foskitt Ct. *North* —1E **17**
Foskitt Wlk. *North* —6E **11**
Fosse Clo. *Well* —4F **33**
Fosse Grn. *Rush* —2G **37**
Foundry St. *North* —4B **14**
Fourth Av. *Well* —2F **33**
Fowey Clo. *Well* —5E **27**
Foxcovert Rd. *North* —2E **11**
Foxendale Sq. *North* —5G **11**
Foxford Clo. *North* —5H **9**
Foxglove Clo. *Rush* —5G **37**

Foxgrove Av. *North* —3H **7**
Fox Hill. *North* —2B **20**
Foxhill Rd. *North* —5G **11**
Foxwell Sq. *North* —1C **10**
Foxwood Clo. *Rush* —3C **36**
Frances Jetty. *North* —4B **14**
Franciscan Clo. *Rush* —5D **36**
Francis Ct. *Rush* —1C **36**
Francis St. *North* —2B **14**
Franklin Cres. *North* —2E **13**
Franklin's Clo. *Ecton* —3H **11**
Franklin St. *North* —3G **13**
Fraser Rd. *North* —1A **10**
Freehold St. *North* —1B **14**
Freeschool St. *North* —4B **14**
Fremeaux Ter. *North* —4A **14**
Frencham Clo. *North* —6G **13**
Friar's Av. *North* —2A **20**
Friars Clo. *North* —2A **20**
Friars Clo. *Well* —2A **34**
Friar's Cres. *North* —2B **20**
Friary, The. *North* —3B **14**
  (off Grosvenor Shop. Cen.)
Frinton Clo. *Rush* —5D **36**
Frosty Hollow. *North* —5B **20**
Fuchsia Clo. *North* —3H **15**
Fulford Dri. *North* —4D **8**
Fulleburn Ct. *North* —4B **10**
Fuller Rd. *Moul* —5H **3**
Fullingdale Rd. *North* —5G **9**
Fulmar La. *Well* —3A **28**
Furber Ct. *North* —3A **10**
Furze Ct. *North* —6H **13**
Furze Rd. *Braf G* —1G **23**
Furze Wlk. *North* —5D **8**
Fylingdale. *North* —2G **7**

Gable Ct. M. *North* —6A **10**
Gadesby Ct. *North* —4B **10**
Gainsborough Dri. *Well* —4H **27**
Galahad Ct. *North* —2B **12**
Galane Clo. *North* —2E **19**
Gallery Clo. *North* —1D **10**
Gallfield Ct. *North* —1F **17**
Galliard Ct. *North* —2E **15**
Gallowhill Rd. *Brac I* —2G **21**
Gambrel Rd. *West I* —3E **13**
Gannet La. *Well* —3A **28**
Gardenfield. *High F* —6F **31**
Garden Fields Ct. *Irch* —5H **35**
Garfield Clo. *North* —4B **8**
Garfield St. *North* —4A **8**
Garrick Rd. *North* —2G **15**
Garrow Clo. *Irth* —1A **30**
Garsdale. *North* —1G **7**
Gas St. *North* —4B **14**
Gatelodge Clo. *Rou S* —1B **10**
Gawaine Ct. *North* —2B **12**
Gayhurst Clo. *Moul* —6G **3**
Gayton Rd. *Blis* —5A **24**
Gedling Clo. *North* —1C **16**
Geldock Rd. *L Bil* —6D **10**
Gentian Clo. *Rush* —5G **37**
George Nutt Ct. *North* —1B **20**
George Row. *North* —4B **14**
George St. *High F* —4G **31**
George St. *Irth* —2C **30**
George St. *Rush* —3F **37**
George St. *Well* —6A **28**
Gervase Sq. *North* —6F **11**
Gibbsacre Ct. *North* —6F **11**
Gibbsacre Wlk. *North* —6F **11**
Gibson La. *North* —1G **13**
Gifford Ct. *North* —1D **12**
Gilbey Clo. *Well* —2G **27**
Gillitts Rd. *Well* —2G **33**
Gillsway. *North* —3H **7**
Gipsy La. *Irch* —5C **34**
Gisburne Rd. *Well* —5A **28**
Glade Clo. *North* —6E **11**
Glade, The. *Well* —2G **27**
Gladstone Clo. *North* —1H **13**
Gladstone Rd. *K Hth* —6H **7**
Glaisdale Clo. *North* —2G **7**
Glamis Clo. *Rush* —4H **37**
Glan y Mor Ter. *North* —2B **8**
Glapthorn Wlk. *North* —2F **11**
Glasgow St. *North* —2G **13**
Glassbrook Rd. *Rush* —3D **36**
Glastonbury Rd. *North* —2B **20**
Glebe Av. *Hard* —3D **20**
Glebe Clo. *Hard* —3D **20**
Glebe Farm Ct. *Gt Dod* —6G **33**
Glebeland Cres. *North* —1G **13**
Glebeland Gdns. *North* —6G **7**
Glebeland Rd. *North* —6G **7**
Glebeland Wlk. *North* —6G **7**

Glebe La. *Gt Hou* —1B **22**
Glebe La. *Pit* —1B **2**
Glebe Rd. *Cog* —3H **17**
Glebe Way. *Cog* —3H **17**
Glebe Way. *Hard* —3D **20**
Glenbank. *Well* —1A **34**
Glendale Ct. *North* —6F **11**
Glendale Wlk. *North* —6F **11**
Gleneagles Dri. *Well* —3F **27**
Glenfield Clo. *Rush* —2D **36**
Glenville. *North* —3G **9**
Gloucester Av. *North* —1A **20**
  (in two parts)
Gloucester Clo. *North* —1A **20**
Gloucester Cres. *North* —1A **20**
Gloucester Cres. *Rush* —2G **37**
Gloucester Pl. *Well* —1A **34**
Godwin Wlk. *North* —5E **7**
Goldcrest Ct. *North* —2D **10**
Goldenash Ct. *North* —3C **10**
Goldings Rd. *North* —2D **10**
Gold Rd. *Well* —6H **27**
Goldsmith Rd. *Well* —1E **33**
Gold St. *North* —4B **14**
Goodens La. *Gt Dod* —6H **33**
Goodwood Av. *North* —3E **9**
Gordon Rd. *Well* —6B **28**
Gordon St. *North* —1B **14**
Gordon St. *Rush* —3D **36**
Gorse Clo. *North* —1A **8**
Gorsehom Ct. *Irth* —2D **30**
Gosforth. *Well* —1E **33**
Goslar, The. *Well* —2D **32**
Goughs Cotts. *North* —2D **12**
Gowerton Rd. *Brac I* —2F **21**
Goy Cres. *North* —3B **14**
Grafton Clo. *North* —4F **27**
Grafton Pl. *Graf S* —2B **14**
Grafton Rd. *Rush* —3H **37**
Grafton St. *North* —2B **14**
Grafton St. Ind. Est. *North* —2A **14**
  (off Grafton St.)
Grafton Vw. *Woot* —5D **20**
Grafton Way. *North* —5C **6**
Grafton Way. *Roth* —4B **18**
Granary Ct. *North* —4B **20**
Granary Rd. *North* —4B **20**
Grange Av. *North* —6C **6**
Grange Clo. *Earls B* —4A **32**
Grange Clo. *Irch* —6H **35**
Grange Rd. *North* —4H **9**
Grange Rd. *Well* —2G **27**
Grange Way. *Irch* —6H **35**
Grangeway. *Rush* —5D **36**
Grangewood. *North* —4H **19**
Grant Rd. *Well* —6B **28**
Grasmere Grn. *North* —1D **32**
Graspin La. *North* —1A **16**
Grasscroft. *North* —2H **7**
Grassmere Av. *North* —5B **10**
Gravely St. *Rush* —3D **36**
Gray Clo. *Earls B* —5C **32**
Gray St. *Irch* —6G **35**
Gray St. *North* —2D **14**
Gt. Billing Pk. *North* —4E **11**
Gt. Billing Way. *North* —2F **11**
Gt. Field Ct. *North* —2B **10**
Gt. Gull Cres. *North* —1C **10**
Gt. Holme Ct. *North* —2B **10**
Greatmeadow. *North* —3F **11**
Greatmeadow Rd. *North* —3E **11**
Gt. Park St. *Well* —6A **28**
Gt. Russell St. *North* —2C **14**
Greaves Clo. *North* —6A **6**
Greenacre Dri. *Rush* —6F **37**
Greenaway Clo. *Blis* —6B **24**
Green Clo. *Well* —4E **27**
Greendale Sq. *North* —5F **11**
Green End. *North* —5A **8**
Greenfield Av. *North* —4F **9**
Greenfield Rd. *North* —4F **9**
Green Fields. *North* —6D **20**
Greenfield Way. *Rush* —4E **37**
Greenfinch Dri. *Moul* —1H **9**
Green Glades. *North* —2F **19**
Greenhills Clo. *North* —1A **8**
Greenhills Rd. *North* —1A **8**
Green La. *North* —2E **19**
Green La. *Woot* —6D **20**
Greenlaw. *Well* —1D **32**
Green Rd. *Braf G* —1H **23**
Greenside. *Blis* —6A **24**
Greenside. *North* —4H **9**
Greenside Gro. *North* —6A **28**
Green St. *Mil M* —1B **24**
Green St. *North* —4A **14**
Green, The. *Braf G* —1H **23**
Green, The. *Gt Hou* —1B **22**

Green, The. *Hard* —3E **21**
Green, The. *K'thpe* —4A **8**
Green, The. *North* —4A **14**
Greenview Dri. *North* —5D **8**
Greenway. *North* —3A **10**
Greenway. *W Fav* —1H **15**
Greenway Av. *North* —3A **10**
Greenwood Clo. *Moul* —5H **3**
Greenwood Rd. *North* —3H **13**
  (in two parts)
Gregory St. *North* —4B **14**
Grendon Wlk. *North* —2E **9**
  (in two parts)
Gresham Dri. *North* —1F **19**
Gretton Clo. *Well* —4F **27**
Greville Av. *North* —3F **9**
Greville Clo. *Bou* —5B **2**
Greyfriars. *North* —4B **14**
Griffin Gdns. *North* —2F **11**
Griffith St. *Rush* —4F **37**
Grimmer Wlk. *Irth* —3B **30**
Grosvenor Gdns. *North* —3C **8**
Grosvenor Shop. Cen. *North* —3B **14**
Groundwell Ct. *North* —6C **10**
Grovebury Dell. *North* —3H **7**
Grove Rd. *Braf G* —6G **17**
Grove Rd. *North* —2D **14**
Grove Rd. *Rush* —3G **37**
Grove St. *High F* —5G **31**
Grove St. *Well* —1G **33**
Grove, The. *Moul* —2H **3**
Guildhall Rd. *North* —4C **14**
Guillemot La. *Well* —4A **28**
Gurston Ri. *North* —3F **11**

Hachenburg Pl. *High F* —6G **31**
Haddon Clo. *Rush* —5E **37**
Haddon Clo. *Well* —3F **27**
Haines Rd. *North* —6B **14**
Hallam Clo. *Moul* —6G **3**
Hall Av. *Rush* —4E **37**
Hall Clo. *North* —3D **12**
Hall Ho. *North* —6G **13**
Hall Piece Clo. *North* —4F **11**
Halswell Ct. *North* —3A **10**
Hambledon Ri. *North* —6F **13**
Hamblin Ct. *Rush* —3F **37**
Hamlet Grn. *North* —1G **13**
Ham Mdw. Dri. *North* —5F **11**
Hammerstone La. *North* —6G **13**
Hampton St. *North* —2A **14**
Hamsterly Pk. *North* —1D **10**
Handcross Way. *Rush* —1G **37**
Handley Clo. *North* —6B **6**
Hanemill Ct. *North* —6F **11**
Hangerfield Ct. *North* —4C **10**
Hanover Ct. *North* —3E **11**
Harborough Rd. *North* —2B **8**
Harborough Rd. *Rush* —4G **37**
Harborough Rd. N. *Pit & Bou* —1A **2**
Harborough Way. *Rush* —4G **37**
Harcourt Sq. *Earls B* —5A **32**
Harcourt Way. *North* —6F **13**
Hardingstone La. *Hard* —3C **20**
Harding Ter. *North* —2B **14**
Hardlands Rd. *North* —1D **12**
  (in two parts)
Hardwick Clo. *Well* —6G **27**
Hardwick Rd. *H'wck & Well* —3B **26**
Hardwick Rd. *North* —3B **20**
Hardwick Rd. *Well* —5E **27**
Hardy Dri. *Hard* —4E **21**
Harebell Sq. *North* —5G **11**
Harefield Rd. *North* —2E **11**
Harefoot Clo. *North* —1C **12**
Harksome Hill. *North* —1F **19**
Harlestone Ct. *North* —2G **13**
Harlestone Ho. *North* —2H **13**
Harlestone Rd. *Harl & North* —1A **6**
Harold St. *North* —3D **14**
Harrier Pk. *North* —4A **28**
Harris Clo. *Woot* —4E **21**
Harrison Clo. *Well* —6F **27**
Harrowden Rd. *Brac I* —1G **21**
Harrowden Rd. *Fin* —1C **28**
Harrowden Rd. *Well* —6B **28**
Harrowick La. *Earls B* —4A **32**
Harrow Way. *North* —1G **7**
Hartburn Ri. *Crow L* —1F **17**
Hartwell Clo. *North* —2C **8**
Harvest Way. *North* —2G **7**
Harvey La. *Moul* —5G **3**
Harvey Reeves Rd. *St James* —4H **13**
Harvey Rd. *Rush* —6F **37**
Harvey Rd. *Well* —2G **33**
Haselrig Sq. *North* —1G **19**
Hassocks Hedge. *North* —1D **18**

Hastings Rd. *North* —3C **8**
Hatfield Clo. *North* —3B **20**
Hatfield Clo. *Well* —4E **27**
Hatton Av. *Well* —6H **27**
Hatton Clo. *Moul I* —1F **9**
Hatton Hall. *Well* —6H **27**
Hatton Pk. Rd. *Well* —6G **27**
Hatton St. *Well* —5H **27**
Havelock St. *Well* —6A **28**
Haven Clo. *North* —2H **13**
Hawkridge. *North* —3G **19**
Hawksbeard Pl. *North* —5F **11**
Hawkshead. *Well* —2D **32**
Hawksmoor Way. *North* —6E **7**
Hawkstone Clo. *Dus* —2E **13**
Hawthorn Rd. *North* —6F **9**
Hawthorns, The. *High F* —5F **31**
Hawthorn Way. *Well* —6G **27**
Hay Clo. *Rush* —5F **37**
Haycroft Wlk. *North* —2H **7**
Hayden Rd. *Rush* —3G **37**
Haydown Grn. *North* —1E **13**
Hayeswood Rd. *North* —3C **10**
Hay La. *Irth* —2C **30**
Hayride, The. *North* —4H **19**
Hayway. *Irth* —2C **30**
Hayway. *Rush* —1E **37**
Hazeldene Rd. *North* —5D **8**
Hazelwood Rd. *North* —4C **14**
Headingley Rd. *Rush* —3H **37**
Headlands, The. *North* —6H **9**
Headlands, The. *Well* —5H **27**
Healey Clo. *North* —3G **11**
Hearden Ct. *Well* —2G **33**
H.E. Bates Way. *Rush* —3D **36**
Heather Ct. *North* —1H **19**
Heather Ct. *Rush* —3E **37**
Heatherdale Way. *North* —4D **8**
Heather La. *North* —3B **10**
Heathfield Boulevd. *North* —3D **14**
Heathfield Way. *K Hth* —5H **7**
Heath Grn. *North* —6G **7**
Heath Ri. *North* —5F **27**
Heathville. *North* —6G **7**
Hecham Way. *High F* —4F **31**
Hedge End. *North* —5B **20**
Hedgely Ct. *North* —1H **19**
Hedgerow Dri. *North* —2H **7**
Hedges, The. *Rush* —1G **37**
Hedge Way. *North* —5B **20**
Hellidon Clo. *North* —3D **8**
Helmdon Cres. *North* —2B **8**
Helmdon Rd. *North* —2B **8**
Hembury Pl. *North* —6G **13**
Hemmingwell Rd. *Well* —4A **28**
Hemmingwell Way. *Well* —4A **28**
Henley Clo. *Well* —5E **27**
Henry St. *North* —2D **14**
Henshaw Rd. *Well* —2F **33**
Herbert St. *North* —3B **14**
Hereward Rd. *North* —1A **20**
Hermitage Way. *North* —5C **20**
  (in two parts)
Hernhill Ct. *North* —1F **19**
Heron Clo. *Well* —4A **28**
Heronsford. *North* —3F **19**
Heron Way. *Well* —4B **28**
Herriotts La. *Well* —6A **28**
Hertford St. *North* —6D **10**
Hervey Clo. *North* —5A **10**
Hervey St. *North* —2D **14**
Hesperus. *Well* —1D **32**
Hester St. *North* —1B **14**
Hever Clo. *Rush* —5G **37**
Hexham Ct. *North* —1H **19**
Hiawatha. *Well* —1D **32**
Hidcote Clo. *North* —4B **20**
Hidcote Clo. *North* —3F **33**
Higgins Sq. *North* —1G **19**
Higham Rd. *L Irch & Irch* —4B **34**
Higham Rd. *Rush* —2F **37**
Highdown Clo. *North* —6F **13**
Highfield Rd. *Irth* —1D **30**
Highfield Rd. *North* —6F **9**
Highfield Rd. *Rush* —4C **36**
Highfield Rd. *Well* —6B **28**
High Greeve. *Woot* —5F **21**
Highgrove Ct. *Rush* —5F **37**
Highlands Av. *North* —3F **9**
High St. *Blis* —6A **24**
High St. *Col* —2F **25**
High St. *Earls B* —5A **32**
High St. *Gt Bil* —5F **11**
High St. *Gt Dod* —6G **33**
High St. *Gt Hou* —6B **16**
High St. *High F* —6F **31**
High St. *Hard* —3D **20**

High St. *Irch* —5H **35**
High St. *Irth* —2C **30**
High St. *K'thpe* —4A **8**
High St. *Mil M* —2B **24**
High St. *Moul* —4H **3**
High St. *Pit* —1B **2**
High St. *Well* —6H **27**
High St. *W Fav* —1A **16**
High St. *Woot* —5C **20**
High St. Pl. *Well* —1H **33**
High St. N. *North* —5B **8**
High St. S. *Rush* —3F **37**
High Vw. *Woot* —5D **20**
Highwoods. *Syw* —5G **5**
Hilberry Ri. *North* —3G **11**
Hillary Rd. *Rush* —4D **36**
Hill Clo. *Lodge F* —5D **6**
Hillcrest Av. *North* —4F **9**
Hilldrop Rd. *North* —4H **19**
Hill Farm Ri. *North* —4H **19**
Hillside Rd. *Well* —4C **28**
Hillside Way. *North* —1H **15**
Hill St. *Well* —1H **33**
Hill, The. *North* —1B **22**
Hind Stile. *High F* —6F **31**
Hinton Clo. *North* —2B **8**
Hinton Rd. *North* —2B **8**
Hirondelle Clo. *North* —6A **6**
Hobby Clo. *North* —3A **20**
Hocknell Clo. *Woot* —5E **21**
Hodnet Clo. *North* —4H **19**
Holbein Gdns. *North* —3F **19**
Holbush Way. *Irth* —1A **30**
Holcot Clo. *Well* —3G **27**
Holcot La. *Syw* —1G **5**
Holcot Rd. *Moul* —1H **3**
Holcutt Clo. *Woot* —4E **21**
Holdenby Rd. *North* —3C **8**
Hollies, The. *Moul* —3G **3**
Hollies, The. *Well* —1G **33**
Hollingside Dri. *North* —4E **9**
Hollow Bank. *Moul* —1H **9**
Hollowell Ct. *North* —1H **33**
Holly Lodge Dri. *North* —2B **8**
Hollyoak Ter. *North* —6A **10**
Holly Rd. *North* —1E **15**
Holly Rd. *Rush* —2C **36**
Holman Clo. *North* —3A **20**
Holme Clo. *Well* —2G **27**
Holmecross Rd. *North* —2B **10**
Holmfield Way. *North* —1H **15**
Holmwood Clo. *North* —6B **6**
Holyrood Rd. *North* —2G **13**
Home Clo. *Blis* —6A **24**
Home Farm Clo. *L Bil* —1E **17**
Homeleigh Clo. *North* —2D **12**
Homestead Ct. *North* —6D **8**
Homestead Ri. *Woot* —5D **20**
Homestead Way. *North* —6D **8**
Honeysuckle Way. *North* —3H **15**
Honister Grn. *North* —4H **9**
Hood St. *North* —2D **12**
Hopes Pl. *K'thpe* —4A **8**
Hopmeadow Ct. *North* —3E **11**
Hopping Hill Gdns. *North* —6D **6**
Hornbeam Clo. *Well* —6G **27**
Hornbeam Ct. *North* —4A **10**
Hornby Rd. *Earls B* —4A **32**
Horse Mkt. *North* —4B **14**
Horsemoor Sq. *North* —5F **11**
Horse Shoe Cotts. *Syw* —2H **5**
Horseshoe St. *North* —4B **14**
Horsewell Ct. *Moul* —6H **3**
Horsley Rd. *North* —6B **8**
Horton Rd. *Braf G* —2G **23**
Houghton Hill. *Hard* —2E **21**
Hove Rd. *Rush* —3G **37**
Howard Biley Gdns. *North* —4H **9**
Howard Ct. Well —6B **28**
  (off Mill Rd.)
Howard La. *Bou* —6B **2**
Hoxton Clo. *North* —1A **10**
Hoylake. *Well* —4E **27**
Hoylake Dri. *North* —4E **9**
Hudson Dri. *North* —2E **19**
Hulme Way. *Well* —4G **27**
Humber Clo. *North* —5F **7**
Humber Gdns. *North* —5E **7**
Humfrey La. *Bou* —5B **2**
Hunsbarrow Rd. *North* —5F **13**
Hunsbury Clo. *North* —2F **19**
Hunsbury Grn. *North* —1F **19**
Hunsbury Hill Av. *North* —6F **13**
Hunsbury Hill Rd. *North* —1F **19**
Hunsbury Wlk. *North* —6G **13**
Hunslet La. *North* —2E **19**
Hunters Clo. *North* —1C **8**

Hunter St. *North* —2C **14**
Huntsham Clo. *North* —2A **16**
Huntsmead. *North* —3G **11**
Huxley Clo. *Well* —1C **32**
Huxloe Ri. *North* —1B **10**
Hyacinth Way. *Rush* —6G **37**
Hybiscus Clo. *North* —3H **15**

Ibstock Clo. *North* —1D **10**
Icknield Dri. *North* —2F **19**
Ilex Clo. *Hard* —2E **21**
Ingleborough Way. *North* —1D **12**
Inglewood Ct. *North* —6F **11**
  (in two parts)
Irchester Cvn. Site. *Irch* —5D **34**
Irchester Rd. *Rush* —3C **36**
Irondale Clo. *North* —6F **13**
Ironstone La. *North* —6F **13**
Irthlingborough Rd. *Well* —2B **34**
Ise Valley Ind. Est. *Well* —3C **28**
Isham Clo. *North* —2C **8**
Ivy Rd. *North* —1E **15**
Ixworth Clo. *North* —2C **10**

Jackdaw Clo. *Crow L* —1F **17**
Jacklin Ct. *Well* —4E **27**
Jackson's La. *Well* —1H **33**
James Lewis Ct. *North* —5H **9**
James Rd. *Well* —3A **34**
James St. *Irch* —6H **35**
Jardine Clo. *North* —6A **10**
Jarretts Yd. *North* —5D **20**
Jasmine Rd. *North* —2F **11**
Jasper Wlk. *North* —1A **10**
Javelin Clo. *North* —1D **12**
Jenner Cres. *North* —2A **8**
Jersey Clo. *Well* —5B **28**
Jersey Ct. *North* —6C **10**
Jeyes Clo. *Moul* —4G **3**
Jeyes Jetty. *North* —4B **14**
Joan Pyel Clo. *Irth* —3C **30**
John Bowen Jones Bus. Pk. *Blis* —3A **24**
John Pyel Rd. *Irth* —2C **30**
John St. *Rush* —3F **37**
John White Clo., The. *High F* —5G **31**
Joshua Sq. *North* —1G **19**
Jubilee Clo. *North* —6G **13**
Jubilee Cres. *Well* —3H **33**
Jubilee Ho. *North* —5B **10**
Jubilee St. *Irth* —1C **30**
Julian Way. *North* —4H **7**
Junction Rd. *North* —6D **8**
Juniper Ct. *North* —4G **11**

Kealdale Rd. *North* —3F **9**
Keats Clo. *Earls B* —5B **32**
Keats Clo. *Gt Hou* —2C **22**
Keats Rd. *Well* —1F **33**
Keats Way. *High F* —6E **31**
Keats Way. *Rush* —2C **36**
Kedleston Rd. *North* —3B **20**
Kelburn Clo. *North* —4A **20**
Kelmscott Clo. *North* —2D **10**
Kelsall Clo. *North* —1C **12**
Kendal Clo. *North* —3A **10**
Kendal Clo. *Rush* —4H **37**
Kendal Clo. *Well* —5E **27**
Kenilworth Clo. *North* —1C **12**
Kenilworth Clo. *Rush* —4G **37**
Kenmuir Av. *North* —5E **9**
Kenmuir Cres. *North* —5E **9**
Kenmuir Gdns. *North* —5E **9**
Kennet Clo. *Well* —5E **27**
Kennet Grn. *North* —5G **7**
Kensington Clo. *Rush* —2C **36**
Kent Clo. *North* —3D **12**
Kentford Clo. *North* —3A **20**
Kent Rd. *North* —2B **12**
Kent Rd. *Rush* —2G **37**
Kent Rd. *Well* —4H **33**
Kentstone Clo. *North* —2G **7**
Kerrfield Est. *North* —2C **12**
Kestrel Clo. *North* —6A **10**
Kestrel La. *North* —3A **28**
Keswick. *Well* —6D **26**
Keswick Dri. *North* —4A **10**
Keswick Dri. *Rush* —2H **37**
Kettering Gdns. *North* —3D **14**
Kettering Rd. *Moul* —4B **4**
Kettering Rd. *North & Spin H* —3D **14**
Kettering Rd. N. *North* —2F **11**
Keyham Ct. *North* —2D **10**
K.G. Bus. Cen. *North* —6G **7**
Kilborn Rd. *Well* —5F **27**
Kilburn Clo. *Well* —4G **27**

Kilburn Pl. *Rush* —1F **37**
Kilby Clo. *Well* —2G **33**
Kilnway. *Well* —4F **27**
Kilvey Rd. *Brac I* —1F **21**
Kimble Clo. *North* —3A **20**
King Cup Clo. *Rush* —6G **37**
King Edward Rd. *North* —2F **15**
Kingfisher Clo. *North* —4H **19**
Kingfisher Ct. *Syw* —5F **5**
King Richard St. *North* —5B **20**
Kings Av. *High F* —4G **31**
Kingscroft Ct. *North* —6F **11**
Kingscroft Wlk. *North* —5F **11**
Kingsfield Bus. Pk. *North* —6H **7**
Kingsfield Clo. *K Hth* —6G **7**
Kingsfield Way. *K Hth* —6G **7**
Kingsland Av. *North* —4B **8**
Kingsland Clo. *North* —4C **8**
Kingsland Gdns. *North* —4B **8**
Kingsley Gdns. *North* —6D **8**
Kingsley Pk. Ter. *North* —6E **9**
Kingsley Rd. *North* —5C **8**
Kingsmead. *North* —2H **7**
Kings Mdw. La. *High F* —3E **31**
King's Rd. *Moul I* —1E **9**
King's Pl. *Rush* —3G **37**
King's Rd. *Rush* —3G **37**
Kings St. *Well* —6A **28**
Kingsthorpe Gro. *North* —5B **8**
Kingsthorpe Ho. *North* —2C **8**
Kingsthorpe Rd. *North* —5B **8**
Kingsthorpe Shop. Cen. *North* —4B **8**
King St. *Earls B* —4A **32**
Kingsway. *North* —3H **7**
Kingsway. *Well* —2F **33**
Kingswell Rd. *North* —4A **8**
Kingswell St. *North* —4B **14**
Kinross Clo. *North* —3F **9**
Kirby Clo. *Woot* —4E **21**
Kirkstone Wlk. *North* —3H **9**
Kirton Clo. *North* —3E **11**
Kislingbury Rd. *Roth* —4A **18**
Kites Clo. *North* —3H **19**
Knaphill Cres. *North* —5G **13**
Knightlands Rd. *North* —1B **30**
Knightley Rd. *North* —6B **8**
Knighton Clo. *North* —4B **6**
Knightscliffe Way. *North* —6E **7**
Knights Clo. *Earls B* —5A **32**
Knights Ct. *L Bil* —6E **11**
Knights Ct. *Well* —6H **27**
Knight's La. *North* —4A **8**
Knowle Clo. *North* —3H **15**
Knowles Clo. *Rush* —2H **37**
Knox Rd. *Well* —1B **34**
Knuston Spinney. *Knu* —4B **36**
Kyle Clo. *North* —6C **8**
Kyoto Clo. *Moul I* —1F **9**

Laburnum Clo. *Well* —6G **27**
Laburnum Cres. *North* —5B **6**
Laceby Wlk. *North* —1C **10**
Ladder Maker Yd. *North* —3B **14**
Ladybridge Dri. *North* —2E **19**
Lady Hollows Dri. *North* —5F **21**
Lady's La. *North* —3B **14**
Ladywell Clo. *Well* —4A **28**
  (nr. Linnet Clo.)
Ladywell Ct. *Well* —4A **28**
  (nr. Robin La.)
Lady Winefride's Wlk. *Gt Bil* —5E **11**
Lakeside. *Irth* —3B **30**
Lakeside Dri. *North* —4G **11**
Lakes, The. *North* —5H **15**
Lakeview Grn. *North* —3H **9**
Lake Wlk. *Col* —1F **25**
Lambrook Dri. *North* —4B **20**
Lancaster St. *High F* —5G **31**
Lancaster Way. *North* —2H **19**
Lancaster Way. *Rush* —2G **37**
Lancum Ho. *Well* —6G **27**
Landcross Dri. *North* —2H **15**
Landor. *Well* —1E **33**
Landsdown Dri. *North* —5B **10**
Lanercost Wlk. *North* —3H **9**
Laneside Hollow. *North* —5B **20**
Lane, The. *Roth* —5C **18**
Langdale Rd. *North* —4C **8**
Langford Dri. *Woot* —6G **20**
Langham Pl. *North* —1B **14**
Langley Clo. *North* —6F **13**
Langsett Clo. *W Fav* —6C **10**
Lapstone Ho. *North* —4H **13**
Lapwing Rd. *North* —4H **19**
Larch Clo. *Irch* —6F **35**
Larch La. *North* —5B **6**

Larchwood Clo. *Well* —6G **27**
Larkhill. *Rush* —1E **37**
Lark Ri. *North* —3D **10**
Larwood Clo. *North* —2H **7**
Lasham Ct. *North* —6F **11**
Lasham Wlk. *North* —6E **11**
Latymer Ct. *North* —3B **14**
Lauderdale Av. *North* —1H **19**
Launcelot Ct. *North* —2B **12**
Laurel Ct. *North* —4B **10**
Laurels, The. *Moul* —4G **3**
Laurel Valley. *North* —1G **25**
Laurence Leyland Complex. Well
  —1D **34**
Lavant Wlk. *North* —2E **9**
Lavender Way. *Rush* —5G **37**
Lavenham Clo. *North* —2C **10**
Lawns, The. *North* —1F **13**
Lawrence St. *North* —2B **14**
Lawson Cres. *North* —6F **11**
Lawton Rd. *Rush* —2G **37**
Laywood Way. *Irth* —3C **30**
Leafields. *North* —1C **16**
Leah Bank. *North* —1H **19**
Lea Rd. *North* —1E **15**
Lea Way. *Well* —1F **33**
Leben Sq. *North* —2F **11**
Ledaig Way. *North* —3F **9**
Lees St. *Irth* —2C **30**
Leicester Pde. North —1B **14**
  (off Barrack Rd.)
Leicester St. *North* —2B **14**
Leicester Ter. *North* —2B **14**
Leighton Pl. *Well* —1H **33**
Leith Ct. *North* —6F **13**
Lennox Wlk. *North* —5E **7**
Leonard La. *Moul* —4H **3**
Leslie Rd. *North* —2A **14**
Letts Rd. *Roth* A —6A **8**
Lewis Rd. *North* —2G **13**
Lexden Clo. *Woot* —4E **21**
Leyland Dri. *North* —2H **7**
Leyland Vw. *Well* —1D **34**
Leys Gdns. *Well* —5B **28**
Leyside Ct. *North* —2E **11**
Leys La. *Gt Hou* —2C **22**
Leys Rd. *Earls B* —5A **32**
Leys Rd. *Well* —6B **28**
Leys, The. *North* —5A **8**
Leyswell Ct. *North* —1D **16**
Liberty Dri. *North* —6D **6**
Lichfield Dri. *North* —4A **20**
Liddington Way. *North* —2B **8**
Lilac Ct. *Well* —6G **27**
Liliput Rd. *Brac I* —6G **15**
Lilley Ter. *Irth* —1D **30**
Lime Av. *North* —6F **9**
Lime Farm Way. *Gt Hou* —2C **22**
Limefields Way. *North* —5C **20**
Lime Gro. *Well* —4A **28**
Limehurst Clo. *North* —6D **6**
Limehurst Rd. *North* —1D **12**
Limehurst Sq. *North* —1D **12**
Limes, The. *North* —6D **20**
Lime St. *Irth* —1D **30**
Lime St. *Rush* —1F **37**
Lime Ter. *Irth* —1D **30**
Limoges Ct. *North* —5B **6**
Linacre Clo. *North* —1C **10**
Lincoln Rd. *North* —4H **13**
Lincoln St. *North* —4B **8**
Lindale Clo. *North* —4G **9**
Linden Av. *High F* —4F **31**
Linden Ct. *K'thpe* —4A **8**
Linden Rd. *North* —6F **9**
Lindisfarne Way. *North* —3B **20**
Lindsay Av. *North* —5F **9**
Lindsay Ter. *North* —5F **9**
Lingfield Ter. *North* —6E **9**
Lings Way. *North* —2D **10**
Lingswood Pk. *North* —4D **10**
Link Rd. *North* —1H **7**
Link Rd. *Rush* —6F **37**
Links Rd. *Fin R* —3C **28**
Linley Grn. *North* —1E **13**
Linnet Clo. *Well* —4A **28**
Linnetts La. *High F* —6F **31**
Lismore Clo. *Gt Bil* —5F **11**
Lister Dri. *North* —2F **19**
Lister Rd. *Well* —6A **28**
Lit. Billing Way. *North* —5D **10**
Lit. Cross St. *North* —3A **14**
Littledale. *Well*
Lit. Greeve Way. *Woot* —5F **21**
Lit. Gull Clo. *North* —1C **10**
Little La. *Blis* —5A **24**
Little La. *Gt Hou* —1B **22**
Lit. Park St. *Well* —4B **28**

Little St. Rush —4G 37
Littlewood Clo. North —1H 13
Lloyd Clo. Fin R —3B 28
Loach Ct. North —1F 9
Lockcroft Sq. North —5G 11
Lockwood Clo. North —3B 8
Lodge Av. Col —1F 15
Lodge Clo. L Hou —6E 17
Lodge Clo. North —6C 6
Lodge Farm Ind. Est. North —4C 6
Lodge Rd. L Hou —5D 16
Lodge Rd. Rush —5E 37
Lodge Way. Well —4A 28
Lodore Gdns. North —4H 9
Logwell Ct. North —5G 9
Loire Clo. New D —5B 6
Lombardy Ct. North —4A 10
London End. Earls B —5A 32
London End. Irch —6H 35
London Rd. Col —6B 14
London Rd. Well —1A 34
Long Acre. Braf G —6G 17
Longacres. North —3A 20
Longacres Dri. Irth —1A 30
Longfellow Rd. Well —1D 32
Longford Av. L Bil —1D 16
Longland Ct. North —5G 9
Longland Rd. North —5G 9
Longleat Ct. North —3B 20
Long Mallows Ri. North —5F 11
Long Marsh Sq. North —1D 10
Longmead Ct. North —3E 11
Long Mdw. Woot —5F 21
Long Mynd Dri. North —1E 13
Longueville Ct. North —3B 10
Lordswood Clo. Woot —5E 21
Lorne Rd. North —2B 14
Lorraine Cres. North —2G 9
Lorraine Dri. North —2H 9
Loseby Clo. Rush —5E 37
Louise Rd. North —2C 14
Lovat Dri. North —2F 13
Lovell Ct. Irth —1D 30
Lowbury Ct. North —6F 13
Lwr. Adelaide St. North —2B 14
Lwr. Bath St. North —3A 14
Lwr. Cross St. North —3A 14
Lwr. Ecton La. North —1G 17
Lwr. Farm Rd. Moul I —6E 3
Lowergrass Rd. North —6C 10
Lwr. Harding St. North —3B 14
Lwr. Hester St. North —2B 14
Lwr. Meadow Ct. North —2B 10
Lwr. Mounts. North —3C 14
Lwr. Priory St. North —2A 14
Lower Rd. Mil M —1B 24
Lwr. Thrift St. North —3E 15
Low Farm Pl. Moul I —6E 3
Low Greeve. Woot —5F 21
Lowick Clo. Well —4F 27
Lowick Ct. Moul —6H 3
Lowlands Clo. North —6D 6
Lowry Clo. Well —4G 27
Loxton Clo. North —6D 6
Loyd Rd. North —2F 15
Lucas Clo. Irth —3C 30
Ludlow Clo. North —6D 4
Lumbertubs La. North —2H 9
Lumbertubs Ri. North —2A 10
Lumbertubs Way. North —1A 10
Lunchfield Ct. Moul —4H 3
(off Lunchfield La.)
Lunchfield Gdns. Moul —4H 3
Lunchfield La. Moul —4H 3
Lunchfield Wlk. Moul —4H 3
(off Lunchfield Gdns.)
Lutterworth Rd. North —2F 15
Lydia Ct. Rush —3E 37
Lyle Ct. Well —4E 27
Lyncrest Av. North —2F 13
Lyncroft Way. North —6A 8
Lynford Way. Rush —5D 36
Lynmouth Av. North —2H 15
Lynton Av. North —1A 8
Lytham Clo. North —4D 8
Lytham Ct. Well —4E 27
Lyttleton Rd. North —2H 13
Lyveden Rd. Brac I —2F 21

McGibbon Wlk. Irth —3B 30
Maclean Clo. North —2H 15
MacMillan Way. North —3G 9
Macon Clo. North —6A 6
Magee St. North —2E 15
Magnolia Clo. North —3A 14
Maidencastle. North —4E 11

Main Rd. Dus —5C 6
Main Rd. Far C —6H 13
(in two parts)
Malcolm Dri. North —2F 13
Malcolm Rd. North —5E 9
Malcolm Ter. North —5F 9
Malham Ct. Well —5F 27
Mallard Clo. Earls B —4A 32
Mallard Clo. High F —3G 31
Mallard Clo. North —1G 19
Mallery Clo. Rush —2H 37
Mallory Wlk. North —2E 9
Malpas Dri. North —1C 12
Maltings, The. Mil M —1B 24
Malvern Clo. Well —4F 33
Malvern Gro. North —1E 13
Malzor La. Mil M —1B 24
Manfield Rd. North —2F 15
Manfield Way. North —2G 9
Manipur. North —3B 16
Manning Ct. Moul —6H 3
Manning Ri. Rush —4G 37
Manning Rd. Moul —6H 3
Manning St. Rush —4G 37
Mannington Gdns. North —4B 20
Mannock Rd. Well —2G 33
Manor Clo. Gt Har —1F 27
Manor Clo. Irch —5H 35
Manor Dri. Irth —1E 31
Manor Farm Rd. Gt Bil —5E 11
Manorfield Clo. North —1E 17
Manorfield Rd. North —1D 16
Manor Ho. Clo. Earls B —5A 32
Manor Rd. Earls B —4A 32
Manor Rd. Moul —5H 3
Manor Rd. North —4A 8
Manor Rd. Pit —1C 2
Manor Rd. Rush —6F 37
Manor Way. High F —6G 31
Mansard Clo. West I —3F 13
Mansion Clo. Moul I —1F 9
Manton Rd. Irth —1C 30
Manton Rd. Rush —4G 37
Maple Dri. Well —6G 27
Maple Rd. Rush —3G 37
Maple St. North —2B 14
Maple Wood. Rush —6F 37
Mapperley Dri. North —1C 16
Marble Arch. North —2B 14
Marchwood Clo. North —1C 10
Mare Fair. North —4A 14
Margaret Av. Well —3G 33
Margaret St. North —2C 14
Marjoram Clo. North —5C 20
Market Cross. Irth —1D 30
Market Sq. High F —6G 31
Market Sq. North —3B 14
Market Sq. Well —1A 34
Market St. North —2D 14
(in two parts)
Market St. Well —1A 34
Market Wlk. North —2D 14
Markham Clo. North —6D 6
Marlborough Av. Well —4F 27
Marlborough Rd. North —3H 13
Marlowe Clo. North —4A 20
Marlstones. North —1E 19
Marnock Sq. North —1G 19
Marquee Dri. Riv B —2C 16
Marriott Clo. Irth —3C 30
Marriott St. North —1B 14
Marseilles Clo. North —6A 6
Marsh La. Irth —1E 31
Marshleys Ct. North —2E 11
Marshwell Ct. North —1D 16
Martel Clo. North —1A 12
Martin Clo. Rush —1F 37
Martindale. North —2G 7
Martin's La. Hard —3C 20
Martins Yd. North —2A 14
Marwood Clo. North —2G 15
Masefield Clo. Well —1E 33
Masefield Dri. Rush —3C 36
Masefield Way. North —5D 8
Massey Clo. Hard —3D 20
Matchless Clo. North —6B 6
Mayfield Rd. North —4G 9
Mayor Hold. North —3B 14
Meadow Clo. High F —5E 31
Meadow Clo. North —5C 6
Meadow Clo. Well —4D 28
Meadow Dri. High F —5F 31
Meadow La. L Hou —5D 16
Meadows, The. Well —2G 27
Mdw. Sweet Rd. Rush —6F 37
Meadowvale. Irth —2D 30
Meadow Vw. High F —5E 31
Meadow Vw. North —1G 7

Meadow Wlk. High F —5E 31
Meadow Wlk. Irth —1D 30
Meadow Way. Irth —2D 30
Meadway. North —6A 10
Mears Ashby Rd. Wilby —4D 32
Medbourne Clo. Moul —6G 3
Medellin Hill. North —1C 10
Medinah Clo. North —6C 20
Medway Clo. North —5F 7
Medway Dri. North —5F 7
Medway Dri. Well —5E 27
Medwin. Well —1D 32
Meeting La. Irth —1D 30
Meeting La. North —2D 12
Melbourne Ho. North —3H 13
Melbourne La. North —3D 12
Melbourne Rd. North —3G 13
Melbourne St. North —3E 15
Melbourne Wlk. North —3E 15
Melbury La. North —4E 11
Melbury Pl. North —4E 11
Melchester Clo. Hard —4D 20
Meldon Rd. North —4B 20
Melloway Rd. Rush —3C 36
Melrose Av. North —2F 13
Meltham Clo. North —6C 10
Melton Rd. Well —6C 28
Melton Rd. N. Well —6B 28
Melville St. North —2E 15
Memorial Sq. North —3B 14
Mendip Rd. North —1E 13
Meon Way. North —1E 13
Mercers Row. North —4B 14
Mercia Gdns. North —6H 9
Mercury Dri. Brac I —1F 21
Mere Clo. Braf G —1G 23
Mere Clo. North —3A 20
Merefields. Irth —1A 30
Mere Way. North —4A 20
Merlin Gro. North —3A 20
Merrydale Sq. North —1D 10
Merryhill. North —1F 19
Mershe Clo. Hard —4E 21
Merthyr Rd. North —1E 13
Mescalero. K'thpe —3B 8
Meshaw Cres. North —2G 15
Mews, The. W Fav —1A 16
Micklewell La. North —1C 10
Middle Grass. Irth —1A 30
Middle Greeve. Woot —5F 21
Middlemarch. North —3E 11
Middle Mead Ct. North —6D 10
Middlemore. North —1C 10
Middleton Clo. North —2B 8
Middlewell Ct. North —6C 10
Midfield Ct. North —2B 10
Midland Bus. Cen. High F —5G 31
Midland Rd. High F —5G 31
Midland Rd. Rush —2E 37
Midland Rd. Well —1A 34
Milbury. Earls B —6B 32
Miles Well Ct. North —4A 10
Military Rd. North —2C 14
Millbank. North —5G 11
Millbrook Clo. St James —4H 13
Millerhill. North —1F 19
Millers Clo. Rush —3D 36
Millers La. Well —5H 33
Millers Pk. Well —4A 34
Mill Est. Rush —6F 37
Mill Fields. High F —3F 31
Mill La. Dal & K'thpe —1G 13
Mill La. Sem —2A 14
Mill Mdw. North —2C 8
Mill Rd. North —2B 14
Mill Rd. Well —6B 28
(in two parts)
Mill Rd. Ind. Est. Well —5D 28
Mills Clo. Earls B —5B 32
Millside Clo. North —2C 8
Millstone Clo. North —1E 19
Millway. North —3D 12
Milton Av. North —2E 33
Milton Bri. North —5F 21
Milton Ct. Mil M —2B 24
Milton Rd. L Irch —4C 34
Milton St. High F —6F 31
Milton St. North —6D 8
Milton St. N. North —5D 8
Milverton Cres. North —2H 15
Minerva Way. Well —6F 27
Mitchell Clo. North —5E 7
Moat Pl. North —3A 14
Moffatt Ter. Well —6A 28
Monarch Rd. North —6B 8
Monarch Ter. North —1B 14
Monks Hall Rd. North —2E 15
Monks Pk. Rd. North —2E 15

Monks Pond St. North —3A 14
Monks Way. Well —2A 34
Monmouth Rd. North —2H 13
Montague Cres. North —5E 7
Montague St. Rush —3E 37
Montfort Clo. North —3F 13
Moore St. North —6E 9
Moorfield Sq. North —1D 10
Moorland Clo. North —5B 10
Moorlands. Well —4E 27
Moor Rd. Rush —2E 37
Moray Lodge. North —2C 12
Mordaunt La. North —6E 7
Moreton Av. Well —3F 33
Moreton Way. North —2B 8
Morgan Clo. North —3F 11
Morgan M. North —1G 19
Morris Av. Rush —4D 36
Morris Clo. Park F —5C 26
Morris Rd. North —4C 8
Mortar Pit Rd. North —2F 11
Mortimer Clo. North —1H 19
Mortons Bush. Woot —5E 21
Motspur Dri. North —6A 8
Moulton La. Bou —5B 2
Moulton Pk. Bus. Cen. North —1F 9
Moulton Pk. Ind. Est. North —1F 9
Moulton Rd. Pit —1C 2
Moulton Way. North —1G 9
Moulton Way N. Moul —1H 9
Moulton Way S. Moul —1H 9
Mountclair Ct. North —1B 16
Mountfield Rd. North —1B 30
Mountfield Rd. North —4F 9
Mt. Pleasant. Earls B —5B 32
Mounts Ct. North —4B 10
Muirfield Rd. Well —4E 27
Mulberry Clo. North —2G 13
Mulberry Clo. Well —6G 27
Mumford Dri. Roth —4B 18
Muncaster Gdns. North —4C 20
Murray Av. North —6C 8
Muscott La. North —3C 12
Muscott St. North —3A 14
Museum Way. Riv B —3C 16
Musgrave Clo. Woot —4E 21
Mushroom Fld. Rd. North —5G 11
Musson Clo. Irth —1C 30

Naomi Clo. North —6C 10
Napier Clo. North —1C 32
Narrow La. North —3B 14
Naseby Clo. Well —4F 27
Naseby St. North —1B 14
Navigation Row. North —5B 14
Neale Clo. North —1A 16
Nelson St. North —2B 14
Nene Cen. North —1B 14
Nene Clo. Well —5E 27
Nene Ct. Well —2C 34
Nene Dri. North —5G 7
Nene Ri. Cog —3H 17
Nene Rd. High F —6F 31
Nene Valley Retail Pk. North —5A 14
Nene Valley Way. North —2C 20
Nene Vw. Irth —1D 30
Nene Wlk. North —5G 7
Nene Way. North —5G 7
Nene Way. Upton —5A 12
Nesbitt Clo. North —2B 16
Nest Farm Cres. Well —4A 28
Nest Farm Rd. Well —3A 28
Nest Farm Way. Well —4A 28
Nest La. Well —5B 28
Nether Jackson Ct. North —3E 11
Nether Mead Ct. North —3C 10
Nettle Gap Clo. Woot —5E 21
Newbury Clo. Rush —2H 37
Newby Ct. North —4H 9
Newcombe Rd. North —2H 13
Newcomen Rd. Well —6B 28
Newington Rd. North —3B 8
Newland. North —3B 14
Newland Sq. North —3B 8
Newland Wlk. North —3B 14
(off Grosvenor Shop Cen.)
Newman St. High F —4G 31
Newnham Rd. North —4C 8
Newport Pagnell Rd. Hort —5H 21
Newport Pagnell Rd. Woot —3C 20
Newport Pagnell Rd. W. North —3C 20
Newport Rd. North —2H 13
New Rd. Woot —5D 20
Newstead Clo. North —4G 11
Newstone Cres. North —5F 13
New St. Earls B —5B 32
New St. Irch —5H 35

New St. *Irth* —1D **30**
New St. *Well* —6A **28**
Newton Clo. *Park F* —5D **26**
Newton Rd. *Rush* —4H **37**
Newton Rd. *High F* —5H **31**
Newton Rd. *North* —6D **6**
Newton Rd. *Rush* —3F **37**
Newtown Rd. *L Irch* —4C **34**
Newtown Rd. *North* —3E **15**
Nice Mans. *North* —5C **20**
Nicholas Rd. *Irth* —2C **30**
Nicholas Way. *Rush* —2D **36**
Nicholls Ct. *North* —2B **10**
Nielson Rd. *Fin R* —3C **28**
Nightingale La. *Well* —4B **28**
Niort Way. *Well* —5D **26**
Nippendale. *Rush* —3G **37**
Norfolk St. *North* —1B **16**
Norfolk Ter. *North* —1B **14**
Norman D Gate. *North* —4D **14**
Norman D Gate Ind. Est. *North* —4D **14**
Norman Rd. *North* —6G **9**
Norman Way. *Irch* —5A **36**
Norman Way. *Well* —3F **33**
Normead Sq. *North* —5G **11**
Norris Way. *North* —2C **36**
Norris Way Ind. Est. *Rush* —2C **36**
Northampton La. N. *Moul* —5H **3**
Northampton La. S. *Moul* —1G **9**
Northampton Rd. *Blis* —4A **24**
Northampton Rd. *Cour* —6F **25**
Northampton Rd. *Earls B* —4A **32**
Northampton Rd. *Ecton* —3H **11**
Northampton Rd. *Rush* —2A **36**
Northampton Rd. *Well* —3E **33**
Northcote St. *North* —2A **14**
North End. *High F* —5F **31**
Northen Way. *North* —3G **27**
Northfield Rd. *North* —6C **6**
Northfield Way. *North* —3A **8**
N. Heyes Ct. *North* —2C **10**
N. Holme Ct. *North* —2A **10**
N. Leys Ct. *Moul* —6H **3**
N. Oval. *North* —5G **7**
N. Paddock Ct. *North* —3C **10**
N. Portway Clo. *Rou S* —6C **4**
N. Priors Ct. *North* —3D **10**
North Rd. *Earls B* —4A **32**
North Rd. Way. *North* —1E **9**
North St. *Roth* —5B **18**
North St. *Rush* —2F **37**
North St. *Well* —1H **33**
Northumbria Gdns. *North* —6G **9**
N. Western Av. *North* —3H **7**
Northwood Rd. *North* —5G **9**
Norton Rd. *North* —4B **8**
Notre Dame M. *North* —3C **14**
Nunn Mills Rd. *North* —5D **14**
Nurseries, The. *Moul* —4H **3**
Nursery Dri. *Well* —4B **28**
Nursery Gdns. *Irth* —1C **30**
Nursery La. *North* —5B **8**
Nuthall Clo. *North* —1C **16**

Oak Clo. *Irch* —6G **35**
Oakgrove Pl. *North* —5C **20**
Oakham Clo. *North* —1G **9**
Oakham Clo. *Rush* —5E **37**
Oaklands Dri. *North* —6A **10**
Oakleigh Dri. *North* —6D **6**
Oakley Dri. *Moul* —4A **4**
Oakley Dri. *North* —1F **33**
Oakley Rd. *Rush* —2D **36**
Oakley St. *North* —2C **14**
Oakmont Clo. *North* —6B **20**
Oakpark Clo. *North* —1D **10**
Oakpits Way. *Rush* —4G **37**
Oaks Dri. *High F* —4F **31**
Oak St. *North* —2B **14**
Oak St. *Rush* —1F **37**
Oak Ter. *Irth* —1D **30**
Oak Vw. *Well* —2H **27**
Oak Way. *Irth* —1D **30**
Oakway. *North* —4H **27**
Oakwood Rd. *North* —6E **9**
Oat Hill Dri. *North* —5G **11**
Obelisk Clo. *Bou* —5B **2**
Obelisk Ho. *North* —6B **2**
Obelisk Rd. *North* —6B **2**
Old Barn Ct. *North* —4C **10**
Old Bedford Rd. *North* —5G **15**
Oldenmead Ct. *North* —4C **10**
Olden Rd. *North* —2F **11**
Old Quarry Clo. *North* —3B **10**
Old Towcester Rd. *North* —5B **14**
Old Vineyard, The. *High F* —5F **31**
Old Yew Ct. *North* —4A **8**

Oleander Cres. *North* —3F **11**
Oliver Clo. *Rush* —3G **37**
Oliver St. *North* —6D **8**
Olympia Clo. *North* —3A **20**
Olympic Way. *Well* —6E **27**
Oransay Clo. *Gt Bil* —5F **11**
Orchard Clo. *Mil M* —1B **24**
Orchard Clo. *Rush* —2D **36**
Orchard Clo. *Woot* —5D **20**
Orchard Cotts. *L Hou* —4D **16**
Orchard Grn. *North* —5H **9**
Orchard Hill. *L Bil* —6D **10**
Orchard Ho. *Well* —5A **28**
Orchard Pl. *Irch* —5G **35**
Orchard St. *North* —3H **13**
Orchard Ter. *Well* —1H **33**
Orchard Way. *Cog* —3H **17**
Orchard Way. *North* —3D **12**
Orient Way. *Well* —1A **34**
Orlingbury Rd. *Gt Har* —1F **27**
Orton Rd. *Well* —4F **27**
Orwell Clo. *Well* —5E **27**
Osborn Clo. *Well* —2G **33**
Osborne Clo. *Rush* —1H **37**
Osborne Rd. *North* —5B **8**
Osler Clo. *North* —2A **8**
Osmund Dri. *North* —2D **10**
Osprey La. *Well* —4B **28**
Osprey Ri. *North* —3A **20**
Osprey Vw. *North* —3A **20**
Oswald Rd. *Rush* —3G **37**
Osyth Clo. *Brac I* —1F **21**
Oulton Ri. *North* —2E **9**
Oundle Dri. *Moul* —6G **3**
Ouse Clo. *Well* —6H **27**
Outlaw La. *Well* —6H **27**
Oval Cres. *Rush* —3H **37**
Oval Rd. *Rush* —4H **37**
Overleys Ct. *North* —2E **11**
Overmead Rd. *North* —5F **11**
Overslade Clo. *North* —3H **19**
Overstone Clo. *Moul* —4B **4**
Overstone Cres. *Over* —4E **5**
Overstone La. *Moul* —4B **4**
Overstone La. *North* —2E **11**
(in two parts)
Overstone Rd. *Moul* —4A **4**
Overstone Rd. *North* —3C **14**
Overstone Rd. *Syw* —3F **5**
Overstone Solarium Res. Pk. *Syw*
—5G **5**
Owen Clo. *Well* —6D **26**
Owen Ct. *Braf G* —6H **17**
Owen M. *Well* —6D **26**
Owl Clo. *Moul I* —6E **3**
Oxburgh Ct. *North* —3B **20**
Oxford Clo. *Earls B* —6B **32**
Oxford Ho. *Well* —1H **33**
Oxford St. *North* —6A **14**
Oxford St. *Well* —1H **33**
Oxford St. *Wym* —6E **37**
Oxwich Clo. *Brac I* —2F **21**

Paddock Mill Ct. *North* —3E **11**
Paddocks Rd. *Rush* —2C **36**
Paddocks Way. *L Bil* —6D **10**
Padwell Rd. *North* —1D **16**
Paget Gro. *Gt Hou* —1B **22**
Palk Rd. *Well* —1B **34**
Palmer Clo. *Well* —4F **27**
Palmer Sq. *North* —6F **11**
Palmerston Ct. *North* —3D **14**
Palmerston Rd. *North* —3D **14**
Palm Rd. *Rush* —2C **36**
Parade Bank. *Moul* —4H **3**
Parade, The. *North* —3B **14**
Park Av. *Abing* —1F **15**
Park Av. *Dus* —6B **6**
Park Av. *Rush* —4D **36**
Park Av. N. *North* —5F **9**
Park Av. S. *North* —1F **15**
Park Clo. *Braf G* —1H **23**
Park Clo. *Earls B* —5A **32**
Park Clo. *Syw* —3G **5**
Park Cres. *Well* —6A **28**
Park Cres. E. *North* —5G **7**
Park Cres. W. *North* —5G **7**
Park Dri. *North* —6G **7**
Park Farm Ind. Est. *Well* —5D **26**
(in two parts)
Park Farm Way. *Well* —2C **32**
Parkfield Av. *North* —1B **20**
Parkfield Cres. *North* —1B **20**
Park Hill Rd. *North* —4A **10**
Parklands. *Syw* —4G **5**
Parklands Av. *North* —3F **9**

Parklands Cres. *North* —2F **9**
Park La. *Earls B* —5A **32**
Park La. *North* —6B **6**
Park M. *Well* —6A **28**
Park Pl. *Rush* —3F **37**
Park Rd. *Irth* —2C **30**
Park Rd. *Rush* —3F **37**
Park Rd. *Well* —6A **28**
Parkside. *North* —5G **11**
Park Sq. *North* —5G **7**
Park St. *Earls B* —5A **32**
Park Vw. *Moul* —5B **4**
Park Vw. Clo. *Moul* —4B **4**
Park Wlk. *North* —6G **7**
Parkway. *North* —1A **16**
Parkwood St. *North* —3A **14**
Parracombe Way. *North* —2H **15**
Parsons Meade. *North* —1F **19**
Parsons Pde. *Irth* —1D **30**
Parsons Rd. *Irch* —5H **35**
Partridge Clo. *North* —2H **7**
Parva Ct. *North* —4B **10**
Pasteur Clo. *North* —2A **8**
Pastures, The. *North* —2H **7**
Pastures, The. *Well* —2G **27**
Paterson Rd. *Fin R* —3B **28**
Patterdale Wlk. *North* —3H **9**
Patterson Clo. *North* —6B **10**
Pavilion Dri. *North* —2E **21**
Paxford Clo. *Well* —4G **33**
Paxton Rd. *North* —3A **10**
Peace Clo. *North* —6G **13**
Peacock Pl. *North* —3C **14**
Peacock Way. *North* —3C **14**
Pearmain Av. *Well* —4H **27**
Pearmain Ct. *L Bil* —5D **10**
Pear Tree Clo. *L Bil* —5D **10**
Pebble La. *Well* —1A **34**
Pelham St. *North* —3A **14**
Pell Ct. *North* —4B **10**
Pemberton St. *Rush* —3E **37**
Pembroke Clo. *Rush* —4G **37**
Pembroke Cres. *North* —1H **13**
Pembroke Gdns. *North* —1H **13**
Pembroke Rd. *North* —1H **13**
Penarth Rd. *North* —1H **13**
Pen Ct. *North* —5C **14**
Pendered Rd. *Well* —4A **34**
Pendle Rd. *North* —1D **12**
Penfold Clo. *North* —3A **8**
Penfold Dri. *Gt Bil* —4E **11**
Penfold Gdns. *Rush* —5F **11**
Penfold La. *Gt Bil* —4F **11**
Penistone Rd. *North* —3H **15**
Penistone Wlk. *L Bil* —6C **10**
(nr. Langsett Clo.)
Penistone Wlk. *North* —4B **10**
(nr. Penistone Rd.)
Pennard Rd. *Brac I* —1G **21**
Penn Gdns. *North* —4A **20**
Pennine Way. *North* —2E **13**
Pennycress Pl. *North* —6F **11**
Penrhyn Rd. *North* —6B **14**
Penrith Dri. *Well* —5F **27**
Penvale Rd. *North* —5A **20**
Peppercorn Way. *North* —5C **20**
Perceval Clo. *North* —6E **7**
Percy Rd. *North* —2E **15**
Peregrine Pl. *North* —3H **19**
Perkins Ct. *Well* —6A **28**
Perkins Rd. *Irth* —3C **30**
Perry St. *North* —2E **15**
Pershore Clo. *North* —5G **33**
Pevensey Clo. *Rush* —4H **37**
Peverel's Way. *North* —3F **13**
Peveril Clo. *High F* —5G **31**
Peveril Rd. *North* —2D **12**
Pheasant Way. *North* —2H **7**
Philip Pk. *High F* —6F **31**
Philip Way. *High F* —4G **31**
Phippsville Ct. *North* —6E **9**
Phoenix St. *North* —3B **14**
Piccadilly Clo. *North* —1G **19**
Pie Corner. *Syw* —2G **5**
Pightles Ter. *Rush* —4G **37**
Pightles Wlk. *Rush* —4G **37**
Pike La. *North* —3B **14**
Pikemead Ct. *North* —3E **11**
Pilgrims Pl. *North* —2H **33**
Pilgrim Way. *Well* —2H **33**
Pilton Clo. *North* —2F **11**
Pindar Ri. *North* —1B **10**
Pindar Rd. *North* —4G **33**
Pine Av. *Syw* —4G **5**
Pine Clo. *Irch* —6G **35**
Pine Clo. *Rush* —5E **37**
Pine Copse Clo. *North* —5B **6**
Pine Cres. *Syw* —4G **5**

Pineham Av. *North* —1C **8**
Pine Ridge. *North* —6C **4**
Pine Trees. *North* —6A **10**
Pinewood Rd. *North* —4G **9**
Pipers Clo. *Irth* —1D **30**
Pippin Clo. *Cog* —4H **17**
Pippin Clo. *Rush* —2C **36**
Pippin Clo. Well —1H 33
(off Hill St.)
Pippin La. *L Bil* —5D **10**
Pitsford Rd. *Moul* —3E **3**
Pitstone Rd. *North* —5F **13**
Pitt St. *Well* —1G **33**
Plantagenet Sq. *North* —1G **19**
Pleydell Gdns. *North* —1B **20**
Pleydell Rd. *North* —1B **20**
Plough La. *North* —1H **7**
Ploughmans Wlk. *North* —2A **8**
Plumtree Av. *Well* —4A **28**
Poachers Way. *North* —2A **8**
Poitiers Ct. *North* —6A **6**
Pond Bank. *Blis* —5A **24**
Pond Farm Clo. *North* —2D **12**
Pond Wood Clo. *Moul I* —1G **9**
Poole Rd. *North* —2C **14**
Pope Rd. *Well* —2E **33**
Poplar Clo. *Irch* —6G **35**
Poplar Clo. *Rush* —5E **37**
Poplar Ct. *North* —2A **10**
Poplar St. *Well* —6A **28**
Poppy Clo. *Rush* —5G **37**
Poppyfield Ct. *North* —3C **10**
Porlock Clo. *North* —1F **13**
Portchester Gdns. *North* —1B **16**
Portland Pl. *North* —2D **14**
Portland Rd. *Irth* —1B **30**
Portland Rd. *Rush* —3F **37**
Port Rd. *North* —5B **6**
Portstone Clo. *North* —5B **6**
Pound La. *Gt Bil* —5F **11**
Pound La. *Moul* —4G **3**
Poyntz Gdns. *North* —1F **13**
Poyntz La. *North* —1F **13**
Pratt Rd. *Rush* —3G **37**
Premier Way. *Irth* —3C **30**
Prentice Ct. *North* —2D **10**
Prescott Clo. *North* —3F **11**
Pressland Dri. *High F* —5G **31**
Prestbury Rd. *North* —6B **6**
Preston Ct. *North* —4B **10**
Prestwold Way. *North* —2E **11**
Primrose Hill. North —1B 14
(off Kingsthorpe Rd.)
Primula Clo. *North* —3H **15**
Prince of Wales Row. *Moul* —4A **4**
Princess Clo. *North* —3G **15**
Princess Way. *Well* —3G **33**
Prince St. *Earls B* —4A **32**
Princes Wlk. North —3B 14
(off Grosvenor Shop. Cen.)
Priors Clo. *Rush* —5D **36**
Priory Clo. *North* —3G **15**
Priory Rd. *North* —2H **33**
Priory, The. *North* —3H **15**
Pritchard Clo. *North* —1F **11**
Probyn Clo. *North* —1D **10**
Promenade, The. *Well* —6G **27**
Prospect Av. *Irch* —6F **35**
Prospect Av. *Rush* —1F **37**
Provence Ct. *North* —6A **6**
Purbeck Rd. *Rush* —3B **36**
Purser Rd. *North* —1E **15**
Purvis Rd. *Rush* —3E **37**
Pyghtle, The. *Earls B* —4A **32**
Pyghtle, The. *Well* —5H **27**
Pyghtle Way. *North* —4H **19**
Pyket Way. *North* —1B **16**
Pytchley Ri. *Well* —2F **33**
Pytchley Rd. *North* —2D **36**
Pytchley St. *North* —3D **14**
Pytchley Vw. *Moul* —4A **4**
Pytchley Way. *North* —5C **6**

Quantock Cres. *North* —1E **13**
Quarry Ho. *North* —5B **6**
Quarry Pk. Clo. *Moul I* —1G **9**
Quarry Rd. *North* —5C **6**
Quartercroft. *North* —5B **10**
Quarterstone. *North* —2E **19**
Quebec Rd. *North* —5B **8**
Queen Eleanor Rd. *North* —1A **20**
Queen Eleanor Ter. *North* —1B **20**
Queens Cres. *North* —5C **8**
Queensland Gdns. *North* —5B **8**
Queens Pk. Est. *North* —5A **8**
Queens Pk. Pde. *North* —5B **8**
Queens Rd. *North* —5B **8**

Queen St. *Earls B* —4A **32**
Queen St. *Irth* —1C **30**
Queen St. *Rush* —3F **37**
Queen St. *Well* —1A **34**
Queensway. *High F* —6G **31**
Queensway. *Well* —1E **33**
Queenswood Av. *North* —3H **9**
Quernstone La. *North* —6F **13**
Quinton Rd. *Woot* —6D **20**
Quorn Clo. *Well* —1F **33**
Quorn Rd. *Rush* —2D **36**
Quorn Way. *Graf S* —2A **14**

Racedown. *Well* —2D **32**
Radstone Way. *North* —2B **8**
Raeburn Rd. *North* —5D **8**
Raglan Clo. *Rush* —4H **37**
Raglan St. *North* —3D **14**
Ragsdale Wlk. *North* —1A **10**
Rainsborough Cres. *North* —5G **13**
Raisins Fld. Clo. *North* —4F **11**
Rakestone Clo. *North* —5C **20**
Randall Rd. *North* —6D **8**
Ranelagh Rd. *Well* —6B **28**
Ransome Rd. *North* —6C **14**
Ravensbank. *Rush* —1F **37**
Ravens Cft. *North* —4H **19**
Ravens Way. *Crow L* —1F **17**
Rawley Cres. *North* —6B **6**
Raymond Rd. *North* —2H **13**
Raynsford Rd. *North* —6G **7**
Rea Clo. *North* —4B **20**
Rectory Ct. *Rush* —3F **37**
Rectory Farm Rd. *North* —2F **11**
Rectory La. *Mil M* —2B **24**
Rectory Rd. *Rush* —2F **37**
Redbourne Pk. Ind Est. *North* —6G **15**
Redding Clo. *Rush* —6E **37**
Redhill Way. *Well* —3G **27**
Red Ho. Rd. *Moul I* —6E **3**
Redland Dri. *North* —3H **7**
Redruth Clo. *North* —2A **20**
Redwell Rd. *Well* —5H **27**
Redwing Av. *Moul* —1H **9**
Redwood Clo. *Irch* —6G **35**
Reedham Clo. *North* —6D **6**
Reedhill. *North* —2F **19**
Reedway. *North* —3F **9**
Regal Ct. *Rush* —4G **37**
Regent Sq. *North* —3B **14**
Regent St. *North* —3B **14**
Regent St. *Well* —6A **28**
Reims Ct. *New D* —5B **6**
Rennishaw Way. *North* —4E **9**
Repton Ct. *North* —3A **10**
Resthaven Rd. *Woot* —5C **20**
Restormel Clo. *Rush* —4H **37**
Retford Ct. *North* —3C **10**
Reynard Way. *North* —1C **8**
Reynolds Clo. *Well* —4H **27**
Reynoldston Clo. *Brac I* —2H **21**
Rhosili Rd. *Brac I* —2F **21**
Ribble Clo. *North* —5G **7**
Richmond Clo. *Rush* —5G **37**
Richmond Ter. *North* —3A **14**
Rickyard Rd. *North* —4A **10**
Ride La. *Pit* —1B **2**
Rides Ct. *Moul* —6H **3**
Ridge, The. *Gt Dod* —6G **33**
Ridgewalk. *Gt Bil* —4G **11**
Ridge Wlk. *W Fav* —1B **16**
Ridgeway. *North* —1H **15**
Ridgeway. *Well* —4H **27**
Riding, The. *North* —3C **14**
Riley Clo. *North* —2F **11**
Rillwood Ct. *North* —3B **10**
Ring Way. *North* —6H **13**
Ringwell Clo. *Irth* —1A **30**
Ringwood Clo. *North* —2H **7**
Ripon Clo. *North* —1H **19**
Rise, The. *North* —4A **8**
Riverside Way. *North* —4E **15**
Riverstone Way. *North* —1D **18**
(in two parts)
Riverwell. *North* —5G **11**
Rixon Clo. *North* —6B **10**
Rixon Rd. *Fin R* —3B **28**
Roberts St. *Rush* —3G **37**
Roberts St. *Well* —1G **33**
Robert St. *North* —2C **14**
Robinia Clo. *North* —6F **13**
Robin La. *Well* —4A **28**
Robinson Rd. *Rush* —3G **37**
Rochelle Way. *North* —5B **6**
Roche Way. *Well* —5H **27**
Rockcroft Clo. *North* —5C **20**
Rockingham Ct. *Rush* —5E **37**
Rockingham Rd. *North* —1B **20**
Rock St. *Well* —6H **27**
Roe Rd. *North* —1E **15**
Rokeby Wlk. *North* —6E **7**
Roland Way. *High F* —5F **31**
Roman Way. *Irch* —6H **35**
Romany Rd. *North* —6D **8**
Rookery La. *North* —1H **7**
Rose Av. *Rush* —4D **36**
Roseberry Av. *North* —3G **13**
Rose Ct. Irch —5H 35
(off High St.)
Rosedale Rd. *North* —4C **8**
Roseholme Rd. *North* —2F **15**
Rosemoor Dri. *North* —4B **20**
Rosenella Clo. *North* —6G **13**
Rose Villa. *North* —4E **15**
Rosgill Pl. *North* —5G **9**
Rossette Clo. *North* —1D **12**
Ross Rd. *Wee R* —3F **13**
Rothersthorpe Av. *Roth A* —6H **13**
Rothersthorpe Cres. *Roth A* —6H **13**
Rothersthorpe Rd. *Kis* —3A **18**
Rothersthorpe Rd. *North* —1G **19**
Rothesay Rd. *North* —5E **9**
Rothesay Ter. *North* —5E **9**
Round Spinney Ind. Est. *North* —6B **4**
Rowan Av. *North* —2H **9**
Rowan Clo. *Well* —6G **27**
Rowlandson Clo. *North* —6B **10**
Rowlett Clo. *High F* —6G **31**
Rowtree Rd. *North* —4G **19**
Royal Ter. *North* —2B **14**
Rubble Clo. *Well* —5F **27**
Ruddington Clo. *North* —2B **16**
Rudge M. *North* —1A **12**
Rufford Av. *North* —2B **16**
Runnymede Gdns. *North* —6C **10**
Rushden Rd. *Wym* —6E **37**
Rushmere Av. *North* —3G **15**
Rushmere Cres. *North* —3G **15**
Rushmere Rd. *North* —5F **15**
Rushmere Way. *North* —4G **15**
Rushmere Way. *Rush* —1E **37**
Rushmills. *North* —6G **15**
Rushy End. *North* —5A **20**
Ruskin Av. *Well* —1E **33**
Ruskin Rd. *North* —3B **8**
Russell Ct. *Rush* —3F **37**
Russell Sq. *Moul* —1H **9**
Russell Way. *High F* —5F **31**
Russett Dri. *L Bil* —5D **10**
Rutherford Dri. *Park F* —1C **32**
Rutland Wlk. *Moul* —6G **3**
Rycroft Clo. *Well* —6F **27**
Rydal. *Well* —2D **32**
Rydal Mt. *North* —4H **9**
Rydalside. *North* —6G **13**
Ryder Vw. *Well* —4E **27**
Rydinghurst Stewart Clo. *Moul* —3G **3**
Ryeburn Way. *Well* —6G **27**
Ryebury Hill. *Fin* —1E **29**
Rye Clo. *Rush* —5G **37**
Ryehill Clo. *Lodge F* —5D **6**
Ryehill Ct. *North* —5D **6**
Ryehill Rd. *North* —4C **10**
Ryeland Rd. *Dus* —1B **12**
Ryeland Way. *North* —6B **6**
Ryland Rd. *Moul* —5H **3**
Ryland Rd. *North* —5D **8**
Rylstone, The. *Well* —2D **32**

Saddleback Rd. *West I* —3E **13**
Saddlers Sq. *North* —1C **10**
Saffron Clo. *North* —6C **20**
Saffron Rd. *High F* —4F **31**
(in two parts)
Sage Clo. *North* —3B **10**
St Alban's Clo. *North* —4G **9**
St Alban's Rd. *North* —4G **9**
St Andrews Cres. *Well* —4G **33**
St Andrew's Rd. *North* —4A **14**
St Andrew's St. *North* —3B **14**
St Barnabas St. *Well* —1G **33**
St Benedict's Mt. *North* —2F **19**
St Christopher's Wlk. *North* —2G **15**
St Crispin Av. *Well* —3H **33**
St Crispin Rd. *Earls B* —5B **32**
St David's Rd. *North* —5B **8**
St David's Rd. *Rush* —2B **36**
St Dunstans Ri. *North* —2F **19**
St Edmund's Rd. *North* —3D **14**
St Edmund's St. *North* —3D **14**
St Edmund's Ter. *North* —3D **14**
St Emilion Clo. *North* —6A **6**
St Francis Av. *North* —1H **13**
St George's Av. *North* —1B **14**
St Georges Pl. North —1B 14
(off Kingsthorpe Rd.)
St Georges St. *North* —2B **14**
St George's Way. *Rush* —2D **36**
St Giles Sq. *North* —4C **14**
St Giles St. *North* —4C **14**
St Giles Ter. *North* —3C **14**
St Gregory's Rd. *North* —4A **10**
St James' Clo. *Rush* —1F **37**
St James Mill Bus. Pk. *North* —5G **13**
St James' Mill Rd. *North* —4H **13**
St James' Mill Rd. E. *North* —5A **14**
St James' Pk. Rd. *North* —3H **13**
St James' Retail Pk. *North* —5A **14**
St James' Rd. *North* —3H **13**
St John's Av. *North* —1B **8**
St Johns Clo. *Roth* —5B **18**
St John's St. *North* —4B **14**
St John's St. *Well* —6H **27**
St Julien Clo. *New D* —5B **6**
St Katharine's Way. *Irch* —4G **35**
St Katherine's Ct. North —3A 14
(off Castle Hill)
St Katherine's Sq. *North* —3B **14**
St Katherine's St. *North* —4B **14**
St Leonard's Rd. *North* —6B **14**
St Margarets Av. *Rush* —4D **36**
St Margaret's Gdns. *North* —6G **7**
St Mark's Clo. *Rush* —3C **36**
St Marks Cres. *North* —1A **8**
St Martins Clo. *North* —3B **8**
St Mary's Av. *Rush* —4E **37**
St Mary's Ct. North —3B 14
(off Horsemarket)
St Mary's St. *North* —3B **14**
St Matthew's Pde. *North* —1E **15**
St Michael's Av. *North* —2D **14**
St Michael's Mt. *North* —2D **14**
St Michael's Rd. *North* —3C **14**
St Patrick St. *North* —2B **14**
St Pauls Rd. *North* —1B **14**
St Paul's Ter. *North* —1B **14**
St Peter's Av. *Rush* —3D **36**
St Peter's Gdns. *W Fav* —6A **10**
St Peter's St. *North* —4A **14**
St Peters Wlk. *North* —4B **14**
St Peters Way. *Cog* —3H **17**
St Peter's Way. *Irth* —1D **30**
St Peter's Way. *North* —4A **14**
St Peter's Way Retail Pk. *North* —4B **14**
St Thomas Rd. *Braf G* —6G **17**
Salcey St. *North* —1B **20**
Salem La. *Well* —6H **27**
Salisbury Rd. *Well* —6C **28**
Salisbury St. *North* —1B **14**
Sallow Av. *North* —4F **11**
Salthouse Rd. *Brac I* —1F **21**
Saltwell Sq. *North* —5F **11**
Samwell Way. *North* —2E **19**
Sanders Clo. *Fin R* —3B **28**
Sanders Lodge Ind. Est. *Rush* —2B **36**
Sanders Rd. *Fin R* —2A **28**
Sandfield Clo. *North* —1G **9**
Sandhill Rd. *North* —3H **13**
Sandhills Clo. *North* —1A **8**
Sandhills Rd. *North* —1A **8**
Sandhurst Clo. *North* —3H **19**
Sandiland Rd. *North* —5G **9**
Sandover. *North* —5C **20**
Sandpiper La. *Well* —4A **28**
Sandringham Clo. *North* —2G **15**
Sandringham Clo. *Rush* —4E **37**
Sandringham Clo. *Well* —3F **33**
Sandringham Rd. *North* —2F **15**
Sandy Clo. *Well* —5H **27**
Sandy Hill La. *Moul* —4B **4**
Sandy La. *Harp & North* —3A **12**
Sansom Ct. *North* —4A **10**
Sarek Pk. *North* —4G **19**
Sargeants La. *Col* —1F **25**
Sartoris Rd. *Rush* —3D **36**
Saruman La. *North* —1E **11**
Sasson M. *Well* —6D **26**
Sassoon Clo. *Well* —5D **26**
Sassoon Ct. *Well* —5D **26**
Savill Clo. *North* —4B **20**
Saxby Cres. *Well* —1C **34**
Saxon Lodge. *Earls B* —5A **32**
Saxon Ri. *Earls B* —6A **32**
Saxon Ri. *Irch* —5A **36**
Saxon Ri. *North* —2C **12**
Saxon St. *North* —6G **9**
Scarborough St. *Irth* —1C **30**
Scarletwell St. *North* —3A **14**
Scarletwell Ter. *North* —3A **14**
Scarplands, The. *North* —3D **12**
Scharpwell. *Irth* —1A **30**
Scholars Ct. *North* —4C **14**
School Hill. *Irch* —5H **35**
School La. *Irch* —5G **35**
School La. *Moul* —4H **3**
School Rd. *Irch* —5G **35**
School Way. *North* —5H **9**
Scirocco Clo. *North* —1D **8**
Scotia Clo. *Brac I* —1H **21**
Scotney Clo. *North* —3B **20**
Scotsmere. *Irth* —1A **30**
Scott Rd. *Well* —2E **33**
Seagrave Ct. *North* —2E **11**
Seaton Dri. *North* —6C **10**
Second Av. *Well* —2E **33**
Sedgwick Ct. *North* —4C **10**
Seedfield Clo. *North* —6B **10**
Seedfield Wlk. *North* —1C **16**
Selston Wlk. *North* —2A **16**
Semilong Pl. *North* —2B **14**
Semilong Rd. *North* —2B **14**
Sentinel Rd. *North* —2F **19**
Senwick Dri. *Well* —1C **34**
Senwick Rd. *Well* —1C **34**
Severn Clo. *Well* —5E **27**
Severn Dri. *North* —5G **7**
Seymour St. *North* —3H **13**
Shadowfax Dri. *North* —2E **11**
Shakespeare Rd. *North* —2D **14**
Shakespeare Rd. *Rush* —3C **36**
Shakespeare Rd. *Well* —2D **32**
Shale End. *North* —4B **6**
Shannon Clo. *Rush* —2H **37**
Shap Grn. *North* —3H **9**
Shard Clo. *North* —5B **20**
Sharman Rd. *North* —4H **13**
Sharman Rd. *Well* —1H **33**
Sharrow Pl. *North* —5G **11**
Sharwood Ter. *Irch* —5G **35**
Shatterstone. *North* —5C **20**
Shaw Clo. *Park F* —6D **26**
Sheaf Clo. *Lodge F* —5C **6**
Shearwater La. *Well* —4A **28**
Shedfield Way. *North* —5B **20**
Sheep St. *North* —3B **14**
Sheep St. *Well* —1A **34**
Sheerwater Dri. *North* —4G **11**
Sheffield Way. *Earls B* —6A **32**
Shelford Clo. *North* —2E **11**
Shelley Dri. *High F* —6E **31**
Shelley Rd. *Well* —1D **32**
Shelley St. *North* —6E **9**
Shelsley Dri. *North* —3E **9**
Shepherd Clo. *North* —2H **7**
Shepperton Clo. *Gt Bil* —5F **11**
Sheraton Clo. *North* —5H **9**
Sheriff Rd. *North* —2E **15**
Sherwood Av. *North* —1G **7**
Shipton Way. *Rush* —2A **36**
Shire Pl. *North* —2E **11**
Shirley Rd. *Rush* —2F **37**
Shoal Creek. *North* —6B **20**
Short La. *Well* —6H **27**
Short Stocks. *Rush* —2H **37**
Shurville Clo. *Earls B* —6B **32**
Siddons Way. *Moul* —4A **4**
Sidebrook Ct. *North* —2C **10**
Sidegate La. *Well* —2E **29**
Sidings, The. *Irth* —3B **30**
Silverdale Gro. *Rush* —3C **36**
Silverdale Rd. *North* —5A **10**
Silverstone Clo. *North* —2C **8**
Silver St. *North* —3B **14**
Silver St. *Well* —1A **34**
Simon's Wlk. *North* —3B **14**
Simpson Av. *High F* —4G **31**
Sinclair Dri. *Park F* —5C **26**
Sir John Pascoe Way. *North* —1D **12**
Siward Vw. *North* —5E **7**
Six Acre Wlk. *North* —5F **11**
Skawle Ct. *North* —4C **10**
Skelton Wlk. *North* —3H **9**
Sketty Clo. *Brac I* —2H **21**
Skiddaw Wlk. *North* —3H **9**
Skinner Av. *Upton* —4E **13**
Skinners Hill. *Rush* —3F **37**
Skipton Clo. *North* —4A **20**
Sladeswell Ct. *North* —1C **16**
Slaters Clo. *Rush* —3H **37**
Slips, The. *Gt Har* —1G **27**
Sliptont Wlk. *North* —2F **11**
Smithy, The. *North* —6B **10**
Smyth Ct. *North* —4B **10**
Snapewood Wlk. *North* —3F **11**
Snetterton Clo. *North* —3E **9**
Snowbell Sq. *North* —5F **11**
Somerford Rd. *Well* —5G **27**
Somerset St. *North* —2C **14**
Sotheby Ri. *North* —4G **11**
Southampton Rd. *North* —6B **14**

S. Bern. *North* —6H **13**
S. Bridge Rd. *North* —5C **14**
South Clo. *Rush* —4G **37**
S. Copse. *North* —4A **20**
Southcourt. *Moul* —6G **3**
Southcrest. *North* —2F **19**
Southfield Ho. *North* —3H **13**
Southfield Rd. *North* —2C **12**
Southfields. *Rush* —4G **37**
Southfields Ho. *North* —1D **10**
S. Holme Ct. *North* —2B **10**
Sth. Oval. *North* —6G **7**
S. Paddock Ct. *North* —3C **10**
South Pk. *Rush* —4F **37**
S. Portway Clo. *Rou S* —1C **10**
S. Priors Ct. *North* —4D **10**
South St. *North* —3E **15**
South Ter. *North* —3E **15**
Southwood Hill. *North* —1G **19**
Spanslade Rd. *North* —6D **10**
Sparke Clo. *Well* —4F **27**
Spectacle La. *Moul* —3E **3**
Spelhoe St. *North* —1C **10**
Spencer Bri. Rd. *North* —3H **13**
Spencer Clo. *Earls B* —5B **32**
Spencer Ct. *Rush* —3E **37**
Spencer Haven. *North* —2H **13**
Spencer Pde. *North* —3C **14**
Spencer Rd. *Irth* —2C **30**
Spencer Rd. *North* —2D **14**
Spencer Rd. *Rush* —1E **37**
Spencer St. *North* —4H **13**
Spenfield Ct. *North* —4C **10**
Spey Clo. *Well* —5E **27**
Spinney Clo. *Bou* —6B **2**
Spinney Clo. *Rush* —3D **36**
Spinney Dri. *Col* —1F **25**
Spinney Hill Cres. *North* —3F **9**
Spinney Hill Rd. *North* —3E **9**
Spinney La. *Wilby* —3E **33**
Spinney Rd. *Irth* —1D **30**
Spinney Rd. *North* —1G **9**
Spinney Rd. *Rush* —4D **36**
Spinneyside. *North* —3D **10**
Spinney Ter. *Irth* —1D **30**
Spinney Way. *North* —3F **9**
Sportsmans Clo. *Cog* —3H **17**
Springbanks Way. *North* —3A **20**
Spring Clo. *Bou* —4B **2**
Springer Straight. *North* —6G **13**
Springfield. *North* —3A **16**
Springfield. *Woot* —4D **20**
Springfield Ct. *North* —4C **10**
Springfield Rd. *Rush* —5G **37**
(in two parts)
Spring Gdns. *Earls B* —5B **32**
Spring Gdns. *High F* —5F **31**
Spring Gdns. *North* —4C **14**
Spring Gdns. *Well* —1H **33**
Spring Ho. Well —1H *33*
(off Wood St.)
Spring La. *North* —3A **14**
Spring La. *Well* —1A **34**
Springs, The. *North* —6H **13**
Spring Sth. *Irth* —1D **30**
Spring Ter. *Irth* —1D **30**
Springwood Ct. *North* —2C **10**
Spruce Ct. *North* —4B **10**
Spur Rd. *Well* —4H **33**
Spyglass Hill. *North* —5A **20**
Square, The. *Earls B* —5A **32**
Square, The. *Pit* —1B **2**
Squires Wlk. *North* —4G **9**
Squirrel La. *North* —2D **12**
Stable Ct. *North* —4B **8**
Stafford Pl. *Moul I* —6E **3**
Stagshaw Clo. *North* —3B **20**
Staines Clo. *North* —3F **13**
Standens Barn Rd. *North* —1C **16**
Standing Stones. *Gt Bil* —4E **11**
Stanfield Rd. *North* —3D **12**
Stanford Way. *North* —3B **20**
Stanhope Rd. *North* —6B **8**
Stanley M. *Well* —6B **28**
Stanley Rd. *North* —3H **13**
Stanley Rd. *Well* —6B **28**
Stanley St. *North* —1B **14**
Stanton Av. *North* —3F **9**
Stanton Clo. *Fin R* —3A **28**
Stanwell Way. *Well* —2E **33**
(in two parts)
Stanwick Rd. *High F & Stan* —4G **31**
Starmers Yd. *North* —2D **12**
Station App. *Rush* —2F **37**
Station M. *Gt Bil* —5F **11**
Station Rd. *Blis* —4A **24**
Station Rd. *Cog* —3G **17**
Station Rd. *Earls B* —5A **32**

Station Rd. *Gt Bil* —6F **11**
(in two parts)
Station Rd. *Irch* —5H **35**
Station Rd. *Irth* —1D **30**
(in two parts)
Station Rd. *L Hou* —5D **16**
Station Rd. *Rush* —3E **37**
Steele Rd. *Well* —1F **33**
Steene St. *North* —3H **13**
Stenson St. *North* —3H **13**
Stephen Bennett Clo. *North* —1D **12**
Sterling Clo. *Moul* —4H **3**
Stevens Cl. *Earls B* —4B **32**
Stevenson St. *North* —1B **20**
Stewarts Rd. *Fin R* —2A **28**
Stimpson Av. *North* —1E **15**
Stirling St. *North* —3G **13**
Stockley St. *North* —3D **14**
(in two parts)
Stockmead Rd. *North* —1D **16**
Stocks Hill. Moul —4H *3*
(off Stock St.)
Stockwell Av. *Woot* —6C **20**
Stockwell Rd. *Mil M* —1C **24**
Stockwell Way. *Mil M* —1C **24**
Stoke Firs Clo. *Woot* —5E **21**
Stoke Rd. *Blis* —6A **24**
Stonebridge Ct. *North* —4C **10**
Stonebridge La. *H'wck* —1C **26**
Stone Circ. Rd. *Rou S* —1A **10**
Stone Hill Ct. *North* —4A **10**
Stonelea Rd. *Syw* —2G **5**
Stoneleigh Chase. *North* —6E **7**
Stone Way. *North* —2C **12**
Stonewold Clo. *North* —3H **7**
Stoneyhurst. *North* —6G **13**
Stourhead Dri. *North* —4B **20**
Stour Rd. *North* —3G **13**
Stourton Clo. *Well* —4F **33**
Stow Clo. *Well* —4F **33**
Stowe Wlk. *North* —2E **9**
Stratford Dri. *Woot* —5C **20**
Stratton Clo. *North* —2A **16**
Strawberry Hill. *North* —4F **11**
Straws Wlk. *North* —2C **30**
Straws Yd. *Irth* —2C **30**
Streambank Rd. *North* —1B **10**
Streatfield Rd. *North* —1H **13**
Streeton Way. *Earls B* —4A **32**
Strelley Av. *North* —1C **16**
Strode Rd. *Well* —6B **28**
Stuart Clo. *North* —4G **19**
Stubble Clo. *North* —1H **7**
Stubbs Clo. *North* —4H **27**
Studland Rd. *North* —6A **8**
Sulby Rd. *North* —1B **10**
Sulgrave Rd. *North* —2G **13**
Summerfields. *North* —1F **19**
Summerhouse Rd. *Moul I* —1F **9**
Summit Ri. *North* —4C **20**
Sunderland St. *North* —3H **13**
Sundew Ct. *North* —2E **19**
Sunningdale Clo. *North* —5D **8**
Sunny Side. *Earls B* —5A **32**
Sunnyside. *Ecton* —3H **11**
Sunnyside. *Woot* —5D **20**
Sunset Ct. *L Bil* —5D **10**
Sussex Clo. *North* —3D **12**
Sutton Clo. *North* —4B **10**
Swain Ct. *North* —4B **10**
Swale Dri. *North* —5G **7**
Swale Dri. *Well* —5E **27**
Swallow Clo. *North* —1F **19**
Swallow Dri. *Rush* —1F **37**
Swan La. Well —1A *34*
(off Midland Rd.)
Swansea Cres. *North* —2H **13**
Swansea Rd. *North* —1H **13**
Swansgate Cen., The. *Well* —1A **34**
Swans La. Well —1A *34*
(off Midland Rd.)
Swanspool Clo. *Well* —1A **34**
Swanspool Pde. *Well* —2A **34**
Swan St. *North* —4C **14**
Swans Way. *High F* —3G **31**
Swan Valley Way. *Swan V* —2C **18**
Swan Yd. *North* —3B **14**
Swinburne Rd. *North* —1D **32**
Swinford Hollow. *L Bil* —1D **16**
Sycamore Clo. *Rush* —3G **37**
Sycamore Dri. *Syw* —5G **5**
Sycamore Rd. *North* —2D **12**
Sylmond Gdns. *Rush* —5D **36**
Sylvanus Rd. *Well* —6F **27**
Symington St. *North* —1H **13**
Syresham St. *North* —2B **8**
Sywell Airport Bus. Pk. *Syw* —1H **5**
Sywell Av. *Well* —5F **27**

Sywell Rd. *Park F* —5A **26**
Sywell Rd. *Syw* —4C **4**
Sywell Way. *Well* —5F **27**

Taborley Clo. *North* —6C **10**
Talan Ri. *North* —2E **11**
Talavera Way. *North* —1H **9**
Talbot Rd. *North* —2D **14**
Talbot Rd. *Rush* —4D **36**
Talbot Rd. *Well* —6C **28**
Talbot Rd. N. *Well* —6C **28**
Tall Trees Clo. *North* —3G **19**
Tallyfield End. *North* —6F **13**
Tamar Clo. *North* —5F **7**
Tamarisk Dri. *Moul* —1H **9**
Tanfield La. *North* —4G **15**
Tanglewood. *North* —1G **25**
Tanner St. *North* —4B **14**
Tansy Clo. *North* —2E **19**
Tapeley Gdns. *North* —4C **20**
Tarn Cft. *North* —4G **9**
Tarragon Way. *North* —5C **20**
Tarrant Clo. *Moul* —4A **4**
Tarrant Way. *Moul* —4A **4**
Tate Gro. *Hard* —4D **20**
Tattersall Dri. *North* —3F **9**
Taunton Av. *North* —2H **15**
Tavistock Clo. *North* —5G **11**
Taylor Clo. *Well* —4E **27**
Teal Clo. *High F* —3G **31**
Teal Clo. *North* —3E **19**
Teal La. *Well* —4B **28**
Tebbutt's Yd. *Earls B* —5A **32**
Tees Clo. *North* —5E **27**
Teesdale. *North* —1C **10**
Telford Way. *North* —5E **13**
Templar Dri. *North* —3H **7**
Temple Bar. *North* —2B **14**
Tenby Rd. *North* —1H **13**
Tennyson Clo. *North* —1G **13**
Tennyson Rd. *Rush* —3D **36**
Tennyson Rd. *Well* —2F **33**
Ten Pines. *North* —6C **4**
Tenter Clo. *High F* —6F **31**
Tenter Rd. *Moul I* —6E **3**
Teviot Clo. *North* —5F **7**
Tewkesbury Clo. *North* —2H **19**
Tewkesbury Clo. *Well* —5F **27**
Thames Rd. *North* —4B **20**
Thames Rd. *Well* —5E **27**
Thatchwell Ct. *North* —1C **16**
Thebwell Rd. *North* —6C **10**
Thenford St. *North* —3D **14**
Third Av. *Well* —2F **33**
Thirlestane Cres. *North* —6A **14**
Thirlestane Rd. *North* —6A **14**
Thirlmere. *Well* —6E **27**
Thirlmere Av. *North* —4H **9**
Thistle Ct. *North* —6H **13**
Thistleholme Clo. *North* —4D **8**
Thomas Flawn Rd. *Irth* —3B **30**
Thomas St. North —2C *14*
(off Bailiff St.)
Thomas St. *Well* —6B **28**
Thorburn Rd. *North* —1B **16**
Thornapple Clo. *North* —4F **11**
Thornby Dri. *North* —4A **8**
Thornfield. *North* —3F **11**
Thorn Hill. *North* —6G **13**
Thornton Rd. *North* —6A **8**
Thorpe Clo. *Well* —6E **27**
Thorpe Rd. *Earls B* —4A **32**
Thorpe Rd. *North* —6B **14**
Thorpeville. *Moul* —6A **4**
Three Mile Wlk. *North* —4F **11**
Thrift St. *High F* —6F **31**
Thrift St. *Irch* —5G **35**
Thrupp Bri. *Woot* —5F **21**
Thrush La. *North* —4A **28**
Thruxton Dri. *North* —3E **9**
Thursby Rd. *North* —2G **15**
Thurspit Pl. *North* —5G **11**
Thwaite Wlk. *North* —6D **10**
Thyme Ct. *North* —4B **10**
Tideswell Clo. *North* —3G **19**
Tiffany Gdns. *North* —5B **20**
Tinsley Clo. *North* —4D **8**
Tintagel Clo. *Rush* —5H **37**
Tintern Av. *North* —2H **13**
Tiptoe Clo. *North* —4B **10**
Tithe Barn Rd. *Well* —1A **34**
Tithe Barn Way. *Swan V* —3C **18**
Titley Bawk Av. *Earls B* —3B **32**
Tiverton Av. *North* —6A **2**
Tollbar. *High F* —6F **31**
Tollgate Clo. *North* —5A **8**
Tollgate Way. *North* —3E **13**

Toms Clo. *Col* —2F **25**
Tonmead Rd. *North* —3B **10**
Tonmead Wlk. *North* —4B **10**
Top Mdw. Wlk. *North* —4D **10**
Topwell Ct. *North* —6C **10**
Torrington Cres. *Well* —5G **27**
Torrington Grn. *Well* —5G **27**
Torrington Rd. *Well* —5F **27**
Torrington Way. *Well* —5G **27**
Touraine Clo. *New D* —5A **6**
Towcester Rd. *Mil M & North* —2B **24**
Tower Fld. Sq. *North* —1D **10**
Tower Hill Clo. *North* —6F **13**
Tower St. *North* —3B **14**
Townley Way. *Earls B* —4A **32**
Townsend Clo. *Well* —1H **33**
Townsend Leys. *High F* —3F **31**
Townwell La. *Irch* —5H **35**
Towton Ct. *North* —2H **19**
Trafford Rd. *Rush* —3G **37**
Treetops. *North* —6D **20**
Treetops. *North* —2D **10**
Trelawney. *Well* —6D **26**
Trent Clo. *North* —5F **7**
Trent Clo. *Well* —5E **27**
Tresham Grn. *North* —6E **13**
Trevor Clo. *North* —2F **13**
Trevor Cres. *North* —2F **13**
Trigg Ter. *Well* —1H **33**
Trimley Clo. *North* —3A **16**
Trinity Av. *North* —5C **8**
Trinity Cen. *Park F* —4C **26**
Triumph Gdns. *North* —1A **12**
Trojan Cen. *Fin R* —3A **28**
Troon Cres. *Well* —4E **27**
Troutbeck Wlk. *North* —3H **9**
Trussell Rd. *North* —6F **11**
Tudley Clo. *Woot* —4E **21**
Tudor Rd. *North* —5F **9**
Tudor Wlk. *Rush* —2G **37**
Tudor Way. *Well* —4G **27**
Tulip Dri. *Rush* —6F **37**
Turnberry Ct. *Well* —4E **27**
Turnberry La. *Col* —6B **20**
Turnbrook Clo. *Irth* —1A **30**
Turnells Mill La. *Den I* —4A **34**
Turner Rd. *Well* —4H **27**
Turner St. *North* —2E **15**
Turn Furlong. *North* —2H **7**
Twyford Clo. *L Bil* —1D **16**
Tyebeck Ct. *North* —4A **8**
Tyes Ct. *North* —4C **10**
Tyne Clo. *Well* —5E **27**
Tyne Rd. *Wee R* —3F **13**
Tyringham Clo. *North* —6A **10**

Ullswater Clo. *Well* —6E **27**
Umlow Clo. *North* —6F **13**
Underbank La. *Moul* —1H **9**
Union St. *North* —3C **14**
Upland Rd. *North* —5H **9**
Up. Bath St. *North* —3B **14**
Up. George St. *High F* —4G **31**
Up. Havelock St. *Well* —6A **28**
Up. Kings Av. *High F* —4G **31**
Up. Mounts. *North* —3C **14**
Up. Park Av. *Rush* —4D **36**
Up. Priory St. *Graf S* —2B **14**
Up. Queen St. *North* —2G **37**
Up. Thrift St. *North* —3E **15**
Uppingham St. *North* —2A **14**
Upton Clo. *North* —2C **8**
Upton Way. *North* —4E **13**
Usher Ho. *North* —2C **8**

Valemead Wlk. *North* —3D **10**
(in two parts)
Valentine Way. *Gt Bil* —4F **11**
Vale, The. *North* —6E **9**
Valley Cres. *L Bil* —6E **11**
Valley Rd. *L Bil* —6E **11**
Valley Rd. *North* —3H **33**
Vantage Mdw. *North* —4G **11**
Vardon Clo. *Well* —4E **27**
Varley Clo. *North* —3G **27**
Vaux Rd. *Fin R* —2A **28**
Velocette Way. *North* —6A **6**
Verdant Va. *North* —5C **20**
Vernon St. *North* —3E **15**
Vernon Ter. *North* —3E **15**
Vernon Wlk. *North* —3E **15**
Verwood Clo. *North* —2C **10**
Vicarage Clo. *North* —4H **7**
Vicarage Clo. *Well* —5F **27**
Vicarage Farm Rd. *Well* —5F **27**

Vicarage La. *North* —4H **7**
Vicarage Rd. *North* —2H **13**
Victoria Clo. *Earls B* —4A **32**
Victoria Clo. *Rush* —2F **37**
Victoria Ct. *Rush* —2F **37**
Victoria Gdns. *North* —4C **14**
Victoria Pk. *Den I* —3B **34**
Victoria Promenade. *North* —4C **14**
Victoria Rd. *Cog* —4H **17**
Victoria Rd. *North* —3D **14**
Victoria Rd. *Rush* —2F **37**
Victoria Rd. *Well* —1A **34**
Victoria St. *Earls B* —4B **32**
Victoria St. *Irth* —2C **30**
Victoria St. *North* —3C **14**
Vienne Clo. *North* —1A **12**
Vigo Cres. *North* —4D **14**
Vigo Ter. *North* —4D **14**
Vincent Clo. *North* —1A **12**
Vine Hill Clo. *High F* —5E **31**
Vine Hill Dri. *High F* —5F **31**
Viscount Rd. *North* —1F **11**
Vivian Rd. *Well* —6B **28**
Vokes Clo. *L Bil* —6D **10**
Vyse Rd. *Bou* —6A **2**

Wade Mdw. Ct. *North* —3C **10**
Wade Mdw. Wlk. *North* —4C **10**
Wagtail Clo. *Moul* —6H **3**
Waingrove. *North* —3E **11**
Wakefield. *Well* —1E **33**
Wakefield Rd. *North* —3C **8**
Wakehurst Dri. *North* —4B **20**
Walgrave Clo. *North* —1E **17**
Walker Sq. *Well* —4E **27**
Wallace Gdns. *North* —5E **9**
Wallace Rd. *North* —5E **9**
Wallace Ter. *North* —5E **9**
Wallbeck Clo. *North* —3B **8**
Walledwell Ct. *North* —6C **10**
Wallingford End. *L Bil* —1D **16**
Wallis Clo. *North* —1C **32**
Walmer Clo. *Rush* —4H **37**
Walton Heath Way. *North* —4D **8**
Wansford Wlk. *North* —1B **10**
Wantage Clo. *Moul* —4B **4**
Wantage Rd. *Irch* —5H **35**
Wantage Rd. *North* —1F **15**
Wardington Ct. *North* —3A **8**
Wardlow Clo. *North* —3G **19**
Warmonds Hill. *High F* —6F **31**
Warnham. *North* —6D **26**
Warren Clo. *Irch* —6A **36**
Warren Rd. *North* —2G **13**
Warrens Clo. *Irth* —1D **30**
Warren, The. *Hard* —4E **21**
Warwick Clo. *North* —1C **12**
Warwick Rd. *North* —3A **34**
Washbrook Clo. *L Bil* —6E **11**
Washbrook La. *Ecton* —2H **11**
Washbrook Rd. *Rush* —2E **37**
Washington St. *North* —4A **8**
Waterfowl Wlk. *North* —6E **11**
Watering La. *Col* —1F **25**
Water La. *North* —5D **20**
Waterloo Way. *Irth* —3B **30**
Waterloo Yd. *Well* —1H **33**
Watermeadow Dri. *North* —2C **10**
Waterpump Ct. *North* —2B **10**
Watersmeet. *North* —3G **15**
Waterview Wlk. *North* —2B **10**
Waterworks La. *Well* —4E **27**
Watkin Ter. *North* —5H **7**
Watson Clo. *Well* —4E **27**
Waveney Way. *North* —6D **8**
Waverley Rd. *North* —6D **8**
Waypost Ct. *North* —4C **10**
Wayside Acres. *North* —3A **20**
Weavers Rd. *Well* —1F **33**
Weavers, The. *North* —4B **20**
Webbs La. *Syw* —2F **5**
Weddell Way. *Brac I* —1H **21**
Wedmore Clo. *North* —2E **13**

Weedon Rd. *Harp & Upton* —4A **12**
(in two parts)
Weedon Rd. Ind. Est. *North* —3F **13**
Weggs Farm Rd. *North* —1A **12**
Weir Clo. *Well* —5H **27**
Weldon Clo. *Well* —4F **27**
Welford Rd. *Chu B* —1G **7**
Welland Grn. *North* —5G **7**
Welland Wlk. *North* —5G **7**
Welland Way. *North* —5G **7**
Wellingborough Bus. Cen. *Well* —3B **34**
Wellingborough Rd. *Earls B* —4B **32**
Wellingborough Rd. *Gt Har* —1G **27**
Wellingborough Rd. *Irth* —4H **29**
Wellingborough Rd. *North & Ecton*
—3D **14**
Wellingborough Rd. *Rush* —2B **36**
Wellingborough Rd. *Syw* —2H **5**
Wellingborough Rd. *Well & Fin* —3D **28**
Wellington Ho. *Well* —2C **34**
Wellington St. *North* —3C **14**
Wells Ct. *Moul* —5H **3**
Well Spring. *Blis* —6A **24**
Well Yd. *North* —4A **8**
Wenlock Way. *North* —1E **13**
Wensleydale. *North* —2G **7**
Wentworth Av. *Well* —5E **27**
Wentworth Rd. *Rush* —3E **37**
Wentworth Way. *North* —4D **8**
Wessex Way. *North* —6G **9**
West Bank. *North* —1B **10**
West Brook. *Blis* —5A **24**
Westbrook. *Well* —1D **32**
Westbury Clo. *North* —2E **13**
Westcott Way. *North* —2A **16**
West Cres. *Rush* —3C **36**
Westerdale. *North* —2G **7**
Western Vw. *North* —4A **14**
Western Way. *Well* —2F **33**
Westfield Av. *Rush* —3C **36**
W. Field Pl. *Rush* —3D **36**
Westfield Rd. *Dus* —1C **12**
Westfield Rd. *North* —3G **13**
Westfield Rd. *Well* —1G **33**
Westfields Av. *High F* —6F **31**
Westfields St. *High F* —6F **31**
Westfields Ter. *High F* —6F **31**
Westgate Ind. Est. *North* —3E **13**
Westgate Rd. *North* —3E **13**
Westlea Rd. *Syw* —2G **5**
Westleigh Clo. *North* —1E **15**
W. Leys Ct. *Moul* —6H **3**
W. Mead Ct. *North* —6C **10**
Westminster Rd. *Well* —5F **27**
Westone Av. *North* —6A **10**
Weston Favell Cen. *North* —5C **10**
Weston Mill La. *W Fav* —2B **16**
Weston Way. *North* —1H **15**
Weston Wharf. *North* —4G **13**
W. Oval. *North* —6G **7**
W. Paddock Ct. *North* —3C **10**
W. Priors Ct. *North* —3C **10**
W. Ridge. *North* —4C **8**
W. Rising. *North* —4C **20**
West St. *Earls B* —5A **32**
West St. *Ecton* —4H **11**
West St. *Moul* —4G **3**
West St. *North* —3E **15**
West St. *Rush* —3F **37**
West St. *Well* —1H **33**
West Vw. *L Irch* —4C **34**
Westvilla Cotts. *Well* —1H **33**
W. Villa Rd. *Well* —1H **33**
West Way. *Earls B* —4A **32**
Wetheral Clo. *North* —3H **9**
Whaddon Clo. *North* —2F **19**
Whalley Gro. *Cog* —3H **17**
Wharfe Grn. *North* —5G **7**
Wharf Rd. *High F* —5E **31**
Wheatcroft Gdns. *Rush* —3F **37**
Wheatfield Gdns. *North* —6G **9**
Wheatfield Rd. *North* —6G **9**
Wheatfield Rd. N. *North* —5G **9**
Wheatfield Rd. S. *North* —6G **9**

Wheatfield Ter. *North* —6G **9**
Whernside. *Well* —5F **27**
Whernside Way. *North* —1D **12**
Whilton Rd. *North* —3C **8**
Whistlets Clo. *North* —2E **19**
Whiston Rd. *North* —3C **8**
White Delves. *Well* —4G **27**
White Doe Dri. *Moul* —6H **3**
Whitefield Rd. *North* —6C **6**
Whitefriars. *Rush* —4C **36**
Whitegates. *North* —2E **19**
Whiteheart Clo. *North* —5E **11**
White Hills Cres. *North* —1A **8**
White Hills Way. *North* —1A **8**
White Ho. Ind. Est. *Earls B* —3A **32**
Whiteland Rd. *North* —5H **9**
Whitesands Way. *North* —1D **18**
Whites La. *New D* —4B **6**
Whites Ri. *Irth* —2C **30**
White Vw. *Rush* —3F **37**
White Way. *Earls B* —4A **32**
Whitfield Way. *North* —2E **19**
Whiting Ct. *Moul* —5H **3**
Whittemore Rd. *Rush* —2H **37**
Whittlebury Clo. *North* —2C **8**
Whittle Clo. *Park F* —5D **26**
Whittles Cross. *Woot* —5F **21**
Whitworth Cres. *Earls B* —4A **32**
Whitworth Rd. *North* —2E **15**
Whitworth Rd. *North* —6C **28**
Whitworth Way. *Irth* —3C **30**
Whitworth Way. *North* —3B **34**
Whytewell Rd. *Well* —5H **27**
Wickery Dene. *Woot* —5F **21**
Wilberforce St. *North* —3H **7**
Wilbye Grange. *Well* —3F **33**
Wilby La. *Gt Dod* —6F **33**
Wilby Pk. Mobile Home Pk. *Well* —3E **33**
Wilby St. *North* —3E **15**
Wilby Way. *Well* —3F **33**
Wildacre Rd. *Rush* —3C **36**
Wildern La. *Rush* —6B **20**
Wilford Av. *North* —1C **16**
William Steele Way. *High F* —6G **31**
William St. *North* —2C **14**
Williams Way. *High F* —6F **31**
William Trigg Clo. *Irth* —3C **30**
Williton Clo. *North* —2A **16**
Willow Brook Sq. *North* —4G **11**
Willow Cres. *Gt Hou* —1B **22**
Willow Herb Clo. *Rush* —6G **37**
Willow La. *Gt Hou* —1B **22**
Willow Ri. *L Bil* —1E **17**
Willows, The. *North* —6G **15**
Wilson Cres. *Irth* —2C **30**
Wilson Rd. *Rush* —3E **37**
Wilson Way. *Earls B* —6A **32**
Wimbledon St. *North* —3H **13**
Wimborne Clo. *North* —1A **8**
Wimpole. *Well* —1E **33**
Winchester Clo. *North* —2B **20**
Winchester Rd. *North* —2B **20**
Winchester Rd. *Rush* —4G **37**
Windermere Dri. *Well* —6E **27**
Windermere Way. *North* —3H **9**
Windflower Pl. *North* —5G **11**
Windingbrook La. *Col* —6B **20**
Windmill Av. *Blis* —6A **24**
Windmill Banks. *High F* —4F **31**
Windmill Bus. Cen. *Rush* —3D **36**
Windmill Clo. *Well* —3G **33**
Windmill Rd. *North* —2C **30**
Windmill Rd. *Rush* —3E **37**
Windmill Ter. *North* —3C **8**
Windrush Rd. *Hard* —3E **21**
Windrush Way. *North* —6H **7**
Windsor Ct. *Gt Bil* —5F **11**
Windsor Cres. *North* —3F **13**
Windsor Ho. *North* —1D **12**
Windsor Rd. *Rush* —2G **37**
Windsor Rd. *Well* —4G **33**
Windyridge. *North* —4C **8**
Winnington La. *North* —2F **11**
Winsford Way. *North* —2A **16**

Winstanley Rd. *Well* —1B **34**
Winston Clo. *North* —2H **9**
Wisley Clo. *North* —4B **20**
Wisteria Way. *North* —3H **15**
Witham Grn. *North* —5F **7**
Witham Wlk. *North* —5G **7**
Witham Way. *North* —6G **7**
Witton Rd. *North* —1D **12**
Woburn Ct. *Rush* —5E **37**
Woburn Ga. *North* —4G **11**
Wollaston Rd. *Irch* —6F **35**
Wollaton Gdns. *North* —1C **16**
Woodavens Clo. *North* —2E **19**
Woodborough Gdns. *North* —1B **16**
Woodcote Av. *North* —3E **9**
Woodfields Wlk. *North* —2B **10**
Woodford St. *North* —3D **14**
Woodford Wlk. North —3D **14**
(off Woodford St.)
Woodhall Clo. *North* —2E **19**
Wood Hill. *North* —4C **14**
Woodhill Rd. *North* —6D **6**
Woodland Av. *North* —6F **9**
Woodland Av. *Over* —4E **5**
Woodland Clo. *North* —5C **6**
Woodland Rd. *Rush* —2E **37**
Woodlands Grange. *Earls B* —5C **32**
Woodlands Rd. *Irch* —6F **35**
Woodland Wlk. *North* —1E **11**
Woodley Chase. *North* —6C **6**
Woodpecker Way. *North* —4G **19**
Woodrush Way. *Moul* —6H **3**
Woodside. *Syw* —4G **5**
Woodside Av. *North* —3A **10**
Woodside Cres. *North* —4A **10**
Woodside Grn. *North* —6G **7**
Woodside Wlk. *North* —6F **7**
Woodside Way. *North* —6F **7**
Woodstock. *North* —3D **14**
Woodstock Clo. *Well* —4G **27**
Wood St. *High F* —6G **31**
Wood St. North —3B **14**
(off Grosvenor Shop. Cen.)
Wood St. *North* —1H **33**
Wooldale Rd. *North* —5F **21**
Woolmonger St. *North* —4B **14**
Wooton Hope Dri. *Woot* —4E **21**
Wootton Brook Clo. *North* —5B **20**
Wootton Hall Pk. *Woot* —3C **20**
Wootton Hill Farm. *North* —3G **19**
Worcester Clo. *North* —5E **11**
Wordsworth Rd. *Well* —2D **32**
Wray Wlk. *Rush* —4G **37**
Wrekin Clo. *North* —6F **13**
Wrenbury Rd. *North* —1A **12**
Wroe, The. *High F* —4F **31**
Wychwood Clo. *North* —6B **6**
Wyckley Clo. *Irth* —1A **30**
Wycliffe Rd. *North* —2F **15**
Wye Clo. *North* —5E **27**
Wykeham Rd. *High F* —4G **31**
Wymersley Clo. *Gt Hou* —1C **22**
Wymington Pk. *Rush* —4F **37**
Wymington Rd. *Rush* —6F **37**
Wysall Rd. *North* —2D **10**

Yardley Dri. *North* —1C **8**
Yarrow. *Well* —2D **32**
Yarwell Sq. *North* —1G **19**
Yeldon Ct. *Fin R* —2B **28**
Yelvertoft Rd. *North* —4B **8**
Yeoman Dri. *North* —2A **8**
Yeoman Mdw. *North* —3G **19**
Yewtree Ct. *North* —2A **10**
York Av. *Cog* —4H **17**
York Clo. *High F* —4G **31**
York Rd. *High F* —4G **31**
York Rd. *North* —3C **14**
York Rd. *Rush* —4G **37**
York Rd. *Well* —6B **28**